gardening with light & color

marylyn abbott

with photography by clay perry

gardening with light & color

marylyn abbott

with photography by clay perry

Kyle Cathie Limited

In memory of Una Beatrice Read Abbott
1906 – 1991 who gave me the love of gardens and
Frederick Archibald Abbott
1907 – 1972 who indulged this love

Gardens cannot be achieved without the dedication of those who tend them. Many hands have worked in the gardens at Kennerton Green, Mittagong NSW and at West Green House, near Hartley Wintney, Hampshire and to them I extend my gratitude, especially to David McKinlay whose dedication achieves the great spectacle of flowers each year at Kennerton Green, and Dominic Rendall and his father Mike, who care so well for the garden at West Green House. I remember gratefully Peter and Iris Seagar who built the seaside garden on Dangar Island and Dora Zweck who allowed me to demolish her garden at 'Yaralla' as I made my first tentative gardening attempts.

I must thank Kyle Cathie who suggested I write down my thoughts on trying to garden at either end of the world and her editors, Kirsten Abbott and Charlie Ryrie, who put an amateur's words into an accepted formula. My gratitude also to Geoff Hayes for the inspired design and to Clay Perry for the beautiful photographs of the two gardens.

Clay Perry wishes to thank Elspeth Barker for her black hollyhock, Kate Campbell of Eye Abbey for the euphorbias and tulips, the administrators of Stonecrop Gardens in New York State for the agapanthus, and Thorp Perrow Arborateum for the autumnal acer.

First published in Great Britain 1999 by
Kyle Cathie Limited
122 Arlington Road
London NW1 7HP

Reprinted 2000

ISBN 1 85626 324 X

Text © 1999 Marylyn Abbott
Photography © 1999 Clay Perry

Edited by Kirsten Abbott
Copy-edited by Charlie Ryrie
Design by Geoff Hayes
Production by Lorraine Baird and Sha Huxtable

Marylyn Abbott is hereby identified as the author of this work in accordance with Section 77 of the Copyright, Designs and Patents Act 1988.

A Cataloguing In Publication record for this title is available from the British Library.

Printed and bound in Singapore by KHL Printing Co.

The publishers wish to note that the author photograph on the jacket was taken by Melissa McCord not by John Swannell as credited.

contents

introduction

The phone was ringing as I dragged myself to wakefulness. I saw it was the witching hour and silently cursed the friend who had once again forgotten the world has Time Zones. So it was a rather pained 'hello' that bounced off the satellite to be answered by 'I've found your garden'. Instantly I was fully awake and all was forgiven.

The English summer of 1993 had been a cross-roads year, when realization had come that there was probably only enough time left in my life to undertake one last grand adventure before I gave in and finally learned to play bridge. Like many of my generation I was descended from British pioneers who, although they had been Australians for four generations, still referred to 'the mother country' and were adamant that everything British was best. I had romanced for years about finding the perfect England to live in. It was a colonial's dream of a house surrounded by walls that enclosed formal gardens of some antiquity. Woodlands (bluebell carpeted, naturally), follies, lakes and fields, intersected by chalk streams. It was the Merchant Ivory image of the English countryside, where Jane Austen's Mr Bingley would find comfort and repose.

Fourteen days after that early morning awakening, red-eyed from the long Qantas flight, I pushed open a warped garden gate in Hampshire. There,

emerging from a tendril curtain of hops, was a fine old walled garden. Once formal beds of herbaceous plants now boasted only the strongest of their kind – masses of geranium tangled with waist-high weeds. Two drunken fruit cages stood like sentinels in the bare earth of a former vegetable garden. Box, wobbly with age, formed a jigsaw puzzle in patched-up parterres, and roses, their vigor unrestrained, had crushed whimsical arbors into fragments of trellis.

The crumbling remains of buildings could be glimpsed through a blanket of blackberries. What was the pineapple on top of? Heavens, that emerald green was a lake! Was that an apple tree beneath the brambles and suckers? Never have I been so consumed by desire. This was my garden, and for three long months I waited, turning away from other real estate treasures unearthed from the pages of *Country Life*, waiting for the National Trust to consider my bid to buy the ninety-nine year lease and restore this enchanted place.

Even as my heart claimed this corner of Hampshire my head was saying 'Stop', for on the other side of the world was a charming settler's cottage, surrounded by mature trees and rolling lawns. There new gardens, some still in the planning stage, were being developed alongside a garden that was already part of Australia's

heritage. My horticultural knowledge was of the mother's knee variety, learned in a land where gardeners strove just to make things grow in a climate where days of 30° heat were commonplace and rain fell intermittently during the cold winter months. I knew nothing about gardening in England. Terms such as 'half-hardy plants' fascinated me. What were they? What was this curse with such an appealing name of 'ground elder'? For me, English gardening was a mixture of the Chelsea Flower Show and Rosemary Verey's book *The English Gentlewoman's Garden*.

Looking back I did not even have the sense to be terrified. All I could see was the joy of a totally new life where never would the spade be cleaned and put to rest for winter, for no sooner would one summer pass than I would emerge from a plane into another spring and begin all over again. It is now five years on from those dreaming days, and the gardens of West Green House in Hampshire are cleared, and restoration and replanting begun. At Kennerton Green near Mittagong in New South Wales the new gardens have an air of permanency. I have long since stopped being intrigued that I would garden in gardens half a world apart with 'Green' in their name, and I do not have time to consider what my life would be like if the National Trust had not said 'Yes'.

The god Bacchus, surrounded by the busts of Roman emperors, looks down from the east side of West Green House onto the lawns of the green theater.

The demands of two gardens

Climatically my two gardens are both cool temperate, but each with degrees of extremes in climate. The sometimes frozen soil and long winters of England are more intense than those in Mittagong. The dry winds and long summers in the highlands of New South Wales are foreign to England. This has allowed me the opportunity to watch many of the same plants perform in similar but different soils, climates and latitudes. It is an adventure still only at its beginning but already I am noticing that some plants look more vibrant in England than under Australian skies, and color schemes that in Australia look clear and crisp are positively brash in England.

English friends visiting Australia laugh in amazement at the breakneck pace our plants rush from spring into summer. Within two and a half months from mid-September a range of flowers that gently open over the six months of April to August in England appear nearly all together. The first year I planted my English herbaceous border I wondered what was the matter? Had I purchased unhappy plants? Why were so few flowering? I expected my late daffodils to flower alongside the tulips, bluebells, sparaxis, ranunculus, primulas, Dutch and English iris in the bulb bed to be followed nearly immediately by lilies, forget-me-nots, delphiniums, bearded iris, alstromeria, lupins and penstemons along with the early roses together, just as they would at home.

In Australia I plan for a huge explosion of flowers in wide borders crammed with trees, shrubs and some perennials and lots of early bulbs and annuals. From September to November it is as

'. . . a huge explosion of flowers in wide borders crammed with trees, shrubs and some perennials and lots of early bulbs and annuals.'

flamboyant a mass of flowers as possible, before the deciduous trees darken the beds in dense shade to combat the lack of water and to filter the heat. I plant this way as I simply cannot afford enough water for a midsummer perennial garden. Years ago a special bed was dug alongside a wide green hedge of *Cupressus torulosa*. Here were collected some of the hardiest perennials, asters, catmints, phlox, monarda, achilleas, aquilegias and eryngium amongst many others. They often grew riotously well in early summer, the salvias becoming a blue nightmare as they tried to strangle the entire bed.

But such displays are short lived as inevitably, just before Christmas, along comes an intense wind with searing heat, along with my anger and

frustration as broken, burnt and shrivelled plants have to be cut back before they have properly flowered. Water would allow re-growth but this is not to be for me, and I have learned to accept that an Australian summer in the southern highlands is a time of dense green shade.

So the Hampshire borders are crammed with too many mid-summer plants from an over indulgence in too many plant catalogues. I have never before experienced such an abundance of varieties that allows for every degree of experimentation of color and texture in leaf and flower. But the garden has told me to stop, the atmosphere of this old garden is controlling the planting now, just as the climate in Australia dictates what should be grown there.

Responding to culture

The old walls at West Green House, the long green allées, the surrounding fields and woods, all seem to decide the story the garden should tell. I find I am now using color schemes I would never have contemplated in Australia. Of course England's soft light has much to do with it, a climate that seems to soften all edges with a haze of moisture creates a magic quality of light not even contemplated in the world's driest continent, whatever the latitude.

But my bones say that the accumulated history cannot be ignored in allowing a garden to tell its story. Its civilization cannot be subservient to fashion but begs us to consider the surrounding countryside, its soils and sky, the dictates of its climate, the color of the fences, the style and size of the dominant buildings, the shape of the garden area. Any of these elements can suggest what could be pleasing for the garden. Dig deep into the imagination and create a garden that is right for the environment.

To hear your garden speak through all the tempting plant philosophies available is very difficult. Last summer I fell madly in love with the concept of graded color borders that paid homage to the ideas of two great gardeners – the poet Vita Sackville West and Gertrude Jekyll the painter, both of whom became better known as gardeners. After days of visiting gardens I felt as if the color wheel in flowers had a life of its own and was rolling across the land in a wide ribbon of yellow, blue, purple, red, orange and yellow again, never stopping to look at the passing scene, oblivious to its surroundings.

Similarly the beautiful idea of a totally white garden softened only by plants of greys and greens escaped from Sissinghurst Castle in Kent. This was a stunning concept devised particularly for a gentle landscape, but it captured the imagination of gardeners worldwide. White gardens appeared in every landscape, pristine white flowers were planted on soils of red or volcanic black. With wind and rain these soils lift and the delicate white blooms so often disappear under red or black dust or mud. It is so important to look at the land and recognize its strengths and limitations and to choose colors and plants that will enhance the existing physical landscape.

This is the story of two gardens and what I feel they have told me to do, especially as I choose the colors for my plants. Both gardens at West Green House and Kennerton Green cover about eight acres. Both are country gardens surrounded by farmland, but I fear neither will be allowed to age in peace as both are within an hour and a half from their country's principal cities, an easy trek for garden lovers. It will take wise local councils to protect both these loved and well-visited gardens for the next generation.

However, it is difficult to compare the two gardens. One is truly England: walled gardens, woodlands, lakes and follies all in a historic framework. The other embodies the traditional Australian garden's giant shade trees, too much lawn and meandering garden beds, its existence tied to the amount of water available each summer. In both gardens there have been similar sized spaces to develop. I cannot believe the different solutions I came up with for two spaces the size of a tennis court. Both gardens needed planting around ponds, vegetable gardens and beds along paths, walls and hedges.

I am sure a painter would see the stories of both my gardens in two totally different artistic styles. I wonder if he would see Kennerton Green as a Grandma Moses painting or would he see West Green House as a romantic Gainsborough. Then again would a musician tell a story with the bright sprightly music of Percy Grainger for Kennerton Green and Purcell for West Green House? Would they even remotely feel the layers of history if the gardens and their legends were unknown. By explaining a little of the gardens' histories, I hope when I divulge my ideas on mixing colors you will see where the original thoughts began.

Opposite top: A carefree mix of lavender, mauve and blue bulbs follow the rill down Cherry Walk at Kennerton Green

Opposite below: Dawn sunshine at Kennerton Green

Above: Old walls enclose the garden at West Green House trapping an atmosphere of a bygone age

Previous page: The crumbling remains of a folly in the lakefield at West Green House

West Green's story

Dominic, who is West Green's woodsman, insists he has seen the apparition, on two occasions, coming from the border alongside the allée of yew. Perhaps it is the lone piper who was once said to walk the paths at night playing a lament for Culloden. My favorite West Green story concerns General or 'Hangman' Hawley, the legendary general of the 1745 Rebellion who is said to have built West Green Manor, as it was known until the 1930s. He built the house at the end of a fine avenue of oak trees backed by dark woods, the avenue terminating at the 'Dutch House' owned by a companion in arms a quarter of a mile away. Each evening the two men dined together turnabout in each other's houses. One particular night Hawley headed home from his friend, through a windy black night, and as the horse and rider neared West Green Manor a terrifying shriek was heard. The frightened horse quickened his pace but the banshee noise rose in ever increasing decibels and the terrified animal bolted. Next morning Hawley was found in a ditch beside the road clutching a small cage similar to a lantern containing his friend's frightened parrot!

A bachelor, Hawley died childless and left the Estate to his housekeeper's second son, whose descendants remained for four generations, selling the Estate in the last years of the 19th century. Then came a succession of owners whose pleasure in the house led them to preserve the outer lines and walls of its 18th century garden, while creating their own gardens of unique beauty. First was Dr Playfair who, in 1898, commissioned the brilliant arts and crafts architect Robert Weir Schulz to design a beautiful series of terraces and parterres. These were infilled when Evelyn Duchess of Wellington (always addressed as 'The Duchess' even after remarriage) purchased West Green Manor in 1905 and established within the existing framework gardens that were worthy enough for praise from a *Country Life* article on 21 November 1936 'Looking back at the house…[one] confronts once more the four Roman emperors with wisteria draped over them weeping for their sins.'

About this time, into the story came Evonne FitzRoy whose remarkable life rivals that of any of the great early adventuresses. She was a voluntary nurse in Eastern Europe who was caught up in the Russian Revolution on returning home in 1916. As secretary to Lady Redding, the wife of the Viceroy of India, she met Gandhi on his first visit to the British Head of State. For good measure she motored across the width of Canada in a small car with a 'spinster' friend. To assist the financially

The notorious General Hawley who built West Green House. During his life it was rumored that he was the son of George Lewis, son of the Elector of Hanover who was to become George I

troubled duchess she persuaded her friend Sir Victor Sassoon to purchase West Green House (the name changed from Manor in the 1930s), on the understanding that it would be home for life for the duchess and herself.

Following Miss Fitzroy's death it became the turn of the great collector Lord McAlpine to add his flourish to the old house at West Green, when he became the first tenant for the National Trust. With the neoclassical architect Quinlan Terry, McAlpine built some of the 20th century's most important garden follies, creating a landscape of innovative architecture in the field surrounding what was still in essence an 18th century garden. The Nymphaeum – a folly based on a Roman fountain – whimsical birdcages, temples and a grotto were constructed surrounding a lake which was inhabited by flamingoes and rare birds, while obscure breeds of cattle and sheep grazed the pasture. A new double avenue of lime trees was punctuated by a column with a Latin inscription that reads 'This monument was built with a large sum of money which would have otherwise fallen, sooner or later, into the hands of the tax gatherer'.

After McAlpine's tenancy the garden was left to quietly crumble into disarray beneath rampant roses to create the picturesque in gardening. But in early 1990 disaster hit the old house, for a bomb planted by the IRA exploded, some months after McAlpine, then an outspoken Conservative party treasurer, had relinquished the lease. The damage was severe and the question was asked if the house should be repaired or demolished. West Green House was saved but during its years of neglect the garden quietly slipped into a sleeping

Above: Miss Evonne FitzRoy as a young woman

Opposite: The neoclassical architect Quinlan Terry designed the impressive Nymphaeum which today forms the backdrop to a classical water garden

beauty hidden beneath weeds; and brambles became a blanket in time.

At this point of the story I enter and another chapter opens. Spectres, duchesses, visionaries, all have left their evidence of occupation of Hawley's Manor in the garden. The terraces of Dr Playfair now form the rake of the Green Theater, the parterre filled with roses in the duchess's time is now rearranged but still entices, and although Lord McAlpine's lakefield of follies is in sad decay they are currently being restored.

Feeling the weight of what had gone before, I felt it impossible to indulge in a fashionable concept of gardening without involving the garden's story in my plans. History creates a special aura which guides me to what garden styles I should choose, which colors will express the story. I have been fortunate in stumbling upon a garden that allows the fun of the grand gesture, and its beauty will absorb fanciful plantings – but only on its own terms.

Kennnerton Green

But this is only half the tale I want to tell for 'down under' is another garden at the opposite end of the spectrum. If a child sat down with some crayons and drew a house, it would probably have a pitched roof with a chimney on top, and a plain front door would be placed in the middle with windows on either side. This simplistic style is the design of an Australian settler's cottage, the first dwellings they made as they moved inland into the bush. Kennerton Green started as such a dwelling, and my garden surrounds a simple house built by a pioneer in the 1860s. It is still basically an unpretentious settler's cottage painted pristine white, rising out of beds of frothy white cottage flowers of picture-book prettiness. The surrounding side-beds are an extension of this cloud of white flowers.

For the past thirty years the garden has been open to visitors each spring. I first came to it on a charity day to see the white flowers and stroll the tree-shaded lawns that surround the house, edging my way into the delightful small rose garden tucked away behind precisely clipped hedges, where old standard roses march in single file along the pond. Wisteria and clouds of all types of blossoms of the palest pink make this an

Right: A dense umbrella of *Wisteria sinensis* frames the colonial settler's cottage at Kennerton Green

Opposite: Every spring plantings of pure white flowers fill the cottage's front borders

Previous page: Tubs of *Azalea* 'Alba Magna' line the back verandah at Kennerton Green

idealized English garden, totally enclosed by a grey-green landscape of eucalyptus.

Australia was settled in 1788, and within twenty years the barrier of the Blue Mountains had been penetrated, and colonists had carved out small farms in the lands beyond. The cool highlands south of Sydney soon became in colonial parlance 'a hill station' where families retreated in December, January and February from the humid coastal heat. Local merchant princes came to the highlands and built grand homes surrounded by splendid gardens that were destined to become household names in polite society.

Along the same road as my cottage, a solid 1900 Federation-style house was built. By the 1950s the elderly owner endowed the main house as a children's home, and moved with his young carer to what is now my cottage. To pass the time the young man started to plant trees, and Ivan 'Snow' Hansen, one of Australia's best-known gardeners, started his career. Although much

smaller than it is today, the garden became part of Australia's gardening heritage during the thirty years that Sir Jock and Lady Pagan spent at Kennerton Green, with 'Snow' Hansen as head gardener. Their preferences set the style that must be incorporated in all I do. My mother and I purchased Kennerton Green in November 1988.

In country Australia the first battle to be fought is to protect the garden from the wind, to ensure a water supply, and to have a good line of prayers to preserve the garden from drought, flood, hot winds and from armies of snails, slugs and grasshoppers. Roses, blossom and setting fruit also need divine protection from flocks of beautiful birds: large white sulphur-crested cockatoos, sugar-pink and grey galahs, scarlet, red and blue mountain lowrys, and the spectacular Rosella parrots whose brilliance is an Australian icon, all are programmed to denude a garden. Kennerton Green answered two prayers: it had mature trees trained into windbreaks along its paddocks, it had

an area where a large dam could be made, and in an emergency, it had access to town water. Surrounding the garden were vast, empty paddocks that were crying out to be included in the planted areas.

Like most gardeners, I took twelve months to watch the original garden through the seasons to understand my land. I needed to imagine what new gardens would flow naturally from the original, and to come to terms with the spirit of the place. As in England the stage for my garden was set by the house, here it was white and simple with the aura of an older Australia. The charm of the house lay in the way it appeared to be nesting amidst its garden so I thought the garden I would plan should revolve around paths always designed to return to the center, an inward looking garden of soft curves inviting a search around a corner gently unfolding its surprises, tall gates that open onto one scene and then another. Allées, grand vistas, and large formal plantings, would have

dwarfed the original dwelling, but I decided to use these elements in more humble form, along with simple plantings in blocks of color, to punctuate the different images I hoped to create.

This book illustrates how I approached two incredibly different gardens at the extremes of architectural design and human aspiration. Both were gardens with their own histories, but both I feel have called to me, one to restore it from nearly terminal ruin, the other to realize its potential. Neither garden is finished and probably will never be.

The Aboriginal people tell us of a dream time when every rock, tree, river and animal, in fact every single thing, has a spirit. I do not disbelieve them. Every garden has its spirit, and it is the gardener's task to interpret this. Gardens must come from their creator's soul. The plants have also been my teachers, their colors in particular have shown me how to set the style and create what I hope is the picture that each garden needs.

'The charm of the house lay in the way it appeared to be nesting amidst its garden . . .'

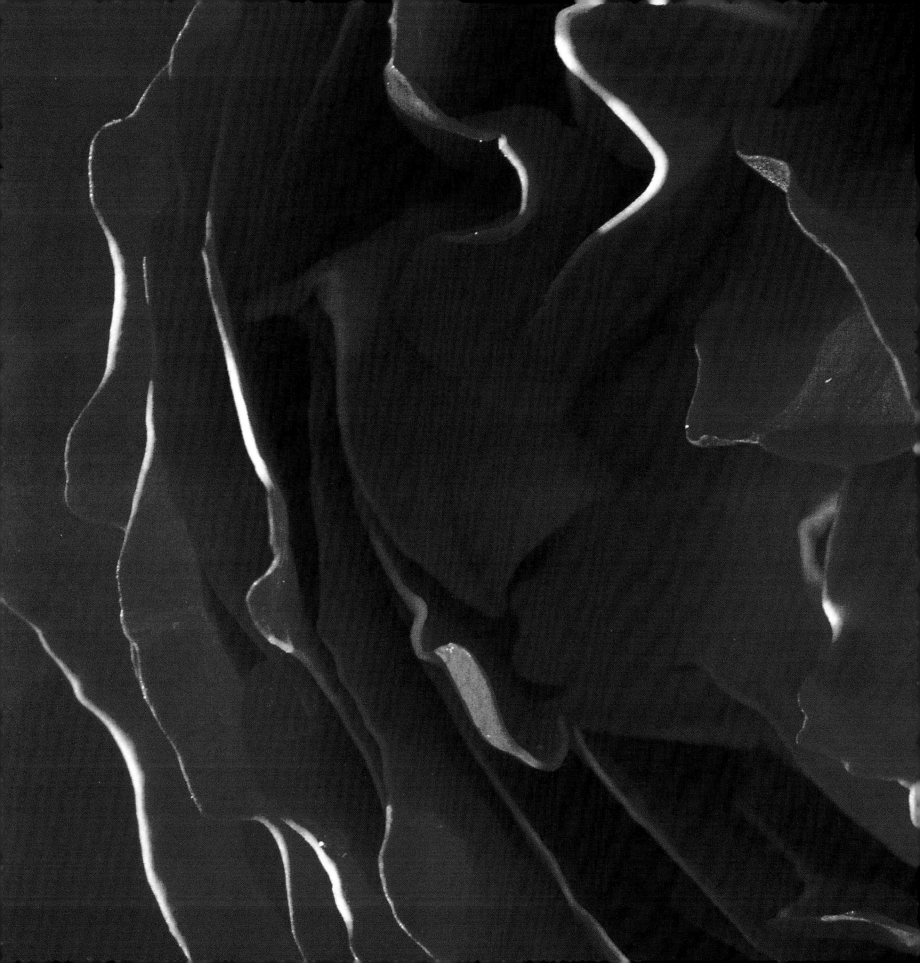

'. . . here there would be a collection of jewel-like plants of ruby, amethyst and sapphire . . .'

Left: Crimson *Rosa* 'Cardinal Hume' with ruby *Dahlia* 'Arabian Night' glow in the 'dark' border at West Green House

Above: *Rosa* 'Charles de Mills'

The moment of truth came in late 1993 when I finally owned my long idealized English garden. I had knowingly placed myself in the epicenter of 20th century gardening, surrounded by gardens considered to be the world's best: within a two hour radius were the gardens of Hidcote, Sissinghurst, Hatfield House, Hadspen and the Royal Horticultural Society Gardens at Wisley – to name just the tip of the iceberg. Moreover, every cool temperate plant I had ever dreamed of growing was available within an hour's drive.

All of a sudden it was indigestible, an over-indulgence in excellence, but luckily the garden saved me, it gave me time to think. It was not ready; I was not ready; I had moved too fast. Dreams on a distant shore are beautiful, but now I had to understand a new climate, landscape, light and hundreds of plants I never knew existed – plants which most of my new friends could give precise Latin names to. The garden was like a beautiful woman of a certain age: the good bones were there but a period of concentrated pampering was needed before the beautiful dress could even be considered. This gave me the breathing space I needed in which to learn.

The first summer was spent tending bonfires as years of neglect were incinerated. My restoration policy was to retain any tree or shrub that could be expected to live, to move any herbaceous plants and bulbs that were salvageable into a newly made nursery area, and to store any hard land-scaping material that we found. I still smile as I remember my first summer when we not only had to clear the borders, but also an amazing area where brambles yielded up trees, follies, temples

and a leaking green lake. I allowed eighteen months for weed eradication and mulching, so when the first plants arrived in the autumn of 1995 we provided them with pampered earth attracting juicy worms, and I had a level playing field to test my skills.

My gardening years at West Green House are simply another chapter in its history, so my ideas can only be gently laid upon an already beautiful, formal structure. But as a gardener steeped in the fashionable 20th century theories of color wheels and saturated color, what was I to do with beds that still contained random lilacs, clumps of the magenta Rugosa rose *Rosa* 'Roseraie de l'Haÿ', a tripod of sugar pink roses and some randomly placed apple trees?

One dusk I entered the main walled garden; late sun played on the warm Hampshire brick walls but the south wall was dramatic and gloomy, a green bank of precision clipped yews, hollies and laurels towered over by cathedral high branches of limes. For a brief moment I caught sight of a flash of red, followed by crimson with an after-glimpse of black blue. It was divine inspiration, for immediately I knew what I wanted to plant in this first border: here there would be a collection of jewel-like plants of ruby, amethyst and sapphire darkly glow-ing as if from the depths of an open treasure box. They would be the colors from the varnished gloom of a baroque ecclesiastical painting, the magenta of a beretta, a red cloak, a purple sash. My clumps of *Rosa* 'Roseraie de l'Haÿ' had inad-vertently shown me that a dark area with poor light needs points of strong, rich color blazing from a shiny background.

Heavy colors in northern light

Conventional wisdom would I believe call for light colors to lift a dark space, but light colors can be very cold, and light clear colors have a modern crispness which was not the feeling I wanted to evoke inside West Green's historic walls, so I opted to use the colors of burgundy, maroon, cerise or magenta. I had never used them before, in fact I had never liked them at all as they are hot heavy colors that capture heat and are totally deadening under the strong white light of summer days in hotter climates. They had always pictured for me the glow in a threatening sky before a ferocious duststorm, the stuffiness of unused parlors, the harsh pink sunsets in dry years that assure us there is no rain on its way.

But in the light of northern latitudes it is so different, deep reds and purples are rich, glamorous colors adding a luxurious allure to color schemes: all of a sudden they became new and exciting.

My plan was not for an exercise in graded or saturated color, but to keep my picture of flashes of baroque jewels. As I searched I was intrigued to find many of these plants already had names inspired by the rich and princely church: *Rosa* 'Cardinal de Richelieu', an old Gallica rose of a rich velvety purple fading to a fine dusty purple as it ages; *Rosa* 'Cardinal Hume', a modern rose of dull crimson purple; *Rosa* 'The Prince', an English rose of the blackest scarlet, and *Rosa* 'Tuscany Superb', a burgundy-crimson velvety Gallica. These were my first choices, and it fast became a treasure hunt for the richest, darkest plants I could find from early spring to late summer. The tulips had similarly

'. . . it fast became a treasure hunt for the richest, darkest plants I could find . . .'

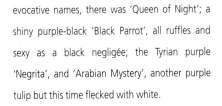

evocative names, there was 'Queen of Night'; a shiny purple-black 'Black Parrot', all ruffles and sexy as a black negligée; the Tyrian purple 'Negrita', and 'Arabian Mystery', another purple tulip but this time flecked with white.

Deep rich colors create their own glamour, but if you have limited space or don't want to devote an entire border to these deep hues, they are spectacular when used to lift other colors or to bring a bland color scheme to life. Dark and poorly lit areas benefit from points of strong rich color, but jewel colors can be equally striking when used in paler beds. There are times when a yellow border, for example, comes to look rather like a pool of melted butter, so add light and contrast with dark jewels and navy blues. The sapphire blue *Agapanthus* 'Midnight Blue', some trumpets of *Hemerocallis* 'Root Beer', the blackest red, and a few spikes of a favorite dark iris will lift a patch of yellow; add a clump or two of the bronze *Rosa* 'Just Joey' to enliven a large border.

Left: Annual *Ranunculus* 'Nearly Black' glow in the warm sunlight

Opposite top left: The shooting stars of *Allium schubertii*

Opposite top right: *Knautia macedonica* – a dark red scabious

Opposite below: Vatican-hued Gallica *Rosa* 'Cardinal de Richelieu'

Form and structure

To give the bed height and weight I planted two *Cotinus coggygria* 'Royal Purple' and five *Berberis thunbergii*, shrubs with burgundy-bronze leaves, and shaped them: the cotinus were shaped into large 4ft (1.2m) round balls and the berberis into small basket balls 3ft (90cm) high to anchor the garden. Between them the tripod – now draped with the very dark crimson climbing *Rosa* 'Guinée', plays host to star-shaped clematis, the velvet red *Clematis* 'Warszawska Nike' with 'Mrs James Mason', double violet-blue and the crimson 'Royal Velvet' with its dark central stripe.

When the short theater of the perennial and annual border is over, clipped shapes add continued interest through their form and structure. Box, bay and yew are all ideal subjects for clipping for all year interest, but with jewel colors cotinus and berberis can be substituted as dramatic statements.

The round shapes of my balls of bronze foliage are echoed in a plant I'm literally sprinkling the garden with, the amethyst-silver balls of *Allium cristophii* which become the stars of the early summer garden, their globes joining this border to the next. The feathery *Anthriscus sylvestris* 'Ravens-wing', black cowparsley with creamy white flowers, is also an early summer plant which is later overtaken by the brighter green foliage of *Astrantia major* 'Ruby Wedding' and its nearly identical cousin *A. major* 'Hadspen Blood', sprinkled with delightful small deep crimson flowers edged in sharp points of petals, striking a slightly deeper note.

Below: An intermingling of ruby red with *Astrantia major* 'Ruby Wedding' and *Lupinus* 'My Castle'

Opposite: The color of old crimson brocade glows from the tall pokers of *Allium sphaerocephalon*

'The sumptuous dark colors evoke a rich past, the ruby brocades on a Georgian wing chair, the deep greens and blues of old tapestry.'

Summer opulence

Irises are essential to fill the flowering gap of early summer, quite a dull time before the perennial border gets underway in earnest. There are many black irises to choose from: I've chosen the blue-black *Iris* 'Black Watch', purple-black *I.* 'Evening Silk' and the violet-blue *I.* 'Dusky Challenger', with *I.* 'Burgundy Bubbles' the exact color of *Rosa* 'Cardinal de Richelieu'. Peonies are another salvation for this time of the year, and I have planted *Paeonia* 'Paul M. Wilde' in this border, a rich red that is rather shy in flowering. The garnet red bearded iris 'Warrior King' will look good nearby in early summer as will the Siberian iris 'Ruffled Velvet', all red-purple and black. Height is supplied by the darkest of delphiniums *D.* 'Black Knight' and the richly purple *Campanula glomerata*. The tall *Allium sphaerocephalon* is a brilliant magenta as autumn approaches, flinging up tall dramatic rods that give a zip to a tiring garden.

My summer color dots are supplied by magenta *Knautia macedonica* and *Lychnis coronaria* 'Magenta', and my exclamation marks are *Atriplex hortensis* var. *Rubra* which grows tall between the rich red dahlia 'Arabian Knight'. It all looks like a late summer Vatican meeting, especially when the dark purple flowers of *Penstemon* 'Burgundy' hang down gently, as though asleep through a long homily on a hot afternoon.

This border is somberly luxuriant most of the season, with melancholy plants including *Sedum atropurpureum*, murky purples and blues trying to shine through a white haze that becomes a bright mass of red-pink flowers in summer, lightening the gloom beside big clumps of the black grass

Ophiopogon planiscapus 'Nigrescens'. *Allium karataviense* pops through as large dusty lavender tennis balls above broad grey green leaves, and to break the somber line I've inserted splashes of the violet-purple bulb *Brodiaea* 'Queen Fabiola', which flowers in midsummer and resembles a small agapanthus while the small growing sapphire *Agapanthus* 'Midnight Blue' adds glamour at the close of summer. Similar in form and structure, but flowering months apart, they ensure a continuity of design in a plant grouping.

The sumptuous dark colors evoke a rich past, the ruby brocades on a Georgian wing chair, the deep greens and blues of old tapestry. They are not the bright, simple colors of Modigliani or a Conran room, but colors of an old landscape. I feel they belong to the history of a house of West Green's age.

Iris are among the most user-friendly of all plants. They perform just as well in the magic of a cool garden, or beside a hot path in Provence. The choicest iris I have ever seen were growing at Junee, outback Australia! After the flamboyance of the tulip and before the summer border really gets going, there is very little at eye-level in the herbaceous border, a gap perfectly filled with iris. Accompany dark colored iris with deep red peonies to achieve several weeks of opulent color. Their contrasting shapes also create a pleasing balance of lightness and stability.

The barely controlled glory of a dazzling clematis clambers over a free-standing tripod

Rich heavy colors

I felt a few brighter reds were needed in my dark bed for summer so I have put in clumps of *Lupinus* 'My Castle', an old brick red to break the overall pall. To continue this color late in the season, I do like the deep rust red of *Sedum* 'Herbstfreude'. Sedums are excellent plants, crisp succulent leaves upright all through the dryest days in pleasing rounded clumps. Then in the last days of summer, they grow and spread flowering with great brilliance, becoming dark sculptural heads in concert with the darkening season.

I would never plant such rich colors together *en masse* at Kennerton Green. When so many of the deep red and purple perennial flowers come into flower the mercury starts to creep to nearly 85° and the plants would look tired and hot, as unsuitable as a heavy velvet robe would be to wear. A Kennerton Green garden answers the heat with deep green and crisp white which could look very stark in dark shade under the pale skies of a cool climate.

Despite their size and structure lupins are equally at home in a small garden – making a proud statement in much the same way as overstuffed furniture can sometimes make a small room look more important. If you only have room for one or two clumps of lupins, try the deep purple-magenta *Lupinus* 'Thundercloud'. Plants choose a gardener just as much as a gardener selects the plants, and lupins do not flourish in every situation, so if you don't succeed with these throw them out and plant something different.

'It all looks like a late summer Vatican meeting, especially when the dark purple flowers of *Penstemon* 'Burgundy' hang down gently, as though asleep through a long homily on a hot afternoon.'

Essential annuals

A garden class came into my garden in mid-summer and were very dismissive of my use of annuals, but I find them essential to fill midseason gaps. The huge bare spot left by late June from clearing away the luxurious *Papaver orientale* 'Patty's Plum' is appropriated by the gloss of *Salpiglossis* 'Chocolate Box', a shiny mixture of purples, dark reds and browns. The velvet *Dianthus barbatus* 'Nigrescens' – absolutely a product of the underworld – needs cutting back by mid-summer, so to have the dark leaved ruby-red *Antirrhinum majus* 'Black Prince' tucked in nearby is a bonus, as it will flower well into the autumn if sown late enough. Other bare spots are filled by the dark red-brown *Cosmos atrosanguineus* and beside the lawn I cram in the black *Viola* 'Midnight Runner'.

Some years I weave a magenta-purple *Cleome* through the center of the bed, its tall stems of 'spider flowers' often reaching 5ft (1.75m) tall. It is a welcome fresh addition to push through rose bushes, tired after the flowering season. Repeatedly I am asked its name to be greeted by disinterest once I say it is an annual.

I do despair of the current anathema to annuals. Of course some are over large and bright, but it is a shame to dismiss all this genus, for beyond the obvious there are gems. I have been accused of being an old testament prophet in my defence of annuals, but I look at my garden in late summer, still flowering brightly, and say a silent prayer of thanks for these wonderful plants. Perhaps in time, they will be resurrected to fashion, like the now acceptable dahlia.

Annuals give enormous flexibility. They are perfect for filling gaps in spring and late summer, little fussed by climate. They are especially useful in smaller gardens planted in groups amongst earlier flowering perennials to introduce more flower as the perennials straggle and fade. In beds with roses and shrubs in the dark jewel colors I carry this color theme into late summer by running the tall magenta cosmos and cleome through the bed and tuck in *Salpiglossis* 'Chocolate Box' at their feet for luscious deep shades. And don't be frightened of dahlias, perfect for late summer brilliance especially those of paint box colors, backed by leaves of bronze they will flower until they die back in horror when touched by the first frost.

'I have been accused of being an old testament prophet in my defence of annuals. .

The old parrot cage surrounded by trees just coming to leaf in the spring time at Kennerton Green

deep jewel-colored favorites

Allium sphaerocephalon

Often called the drumstick allium or the round-headed leek, densely packed fluffy magenta heads appear in late summer at 2-3ft (60-90cm), on thin wiry stems. These easy-to-grow alliums seem to thrive whatever the soil, ideal for growing through low-growing denser plants to provide dramatic outbursts of color above as autumn approaches.

Campanula glomerata 'Superba'

Also known as the clustered bellflower, the wide open bells of this erect 2ft (60cm) tall perennial are deepest violet-purple throughout the summer, providing vivid clumps of color in the middle of a border. This bellflower will grow vigorously in both sun and shade in all but waterlogged soils and is said to be invasive, but I've never found so. If you cut stems back hard after the first flush of flowers, you are rewarded with a second display.

Dahlia 'Arabian Knight'

Largely ignored for decades, dahlias really do deserve more than a second glance, as they provide a perfect injection of color to a late summer border. Nurseryman Nori Pope introduced me to the lovely green foliage and brilliant red flowers of 'Arabian Knight'; flowering from midsummer to the first frosts, reaching 5-6ft (1.5-2m). Plant this variety in rich well-drained soil in groups for vivid splashes of color. All dahlia tubers are frost tender and should be lifted in autumn and replanted after the last frosts in spring, or treat as annuals and reinvest in new tubers each year.

Delphinium 'Black Knight'

If you have room for only one group of jewel-colored spiky plants, choose this delphinium, a majestic 6ft (2m) tall with deep purple flowers and black-purple eyes in early summer. One of the tallest plants in the perennial border, delphiniums must be staked and like fairly rich but well-drained soil. After flowering, cut them right back to encourage a late season showing.

Dianthus barbatus 'Nigrescens'

These glossy blackish-red Sweet Williams shine out from the lower levels of a border in early summer, with foliage as dark as the flower and an intensely sweet and heady scent. Plant them in rich well-drained soil in full sun, and be ruthless and throw plants away to start again when they get straggly as Sweet Williams rarely thrive for more than three or four seasons. Despite this, and their relatively short flowering period, they deserve a place in any garden.

Lupinus 'Thundercloud'

The moody tall, about 3ft (1m), spikes of perennial lupins lift any garden, large or small, but they don't like humidity, and can be a mecca for blackflies and slugs in a damp English summer. In well-drained soils in warmer climates they start to flower in spring through to late summer, in cooler climates you may get a double showing if you cut back the spike after its first summer flowering. 'Thundercloud' is a stunning deep purple and magenta selection.

Rosa 'Cardinal de Richelieu'

No garden should be without its roses. The voluptuous purple-red flowers of this summer flowering Gallica rose fade to a divine dusty purple, perfect in any jewel-colored planting. Compact bushes grow to around 4ft (1.2m). All roses need heavy feeding and mulching to give their best.

Rosa 'Charles de Mills'

I like to train this upright Gallica rose to a tripod or against a wall to make the most of its eager profusion of fragrant double crimson-magenta flowers and mid-green leaves. It happily grows to 5-6ft (1.5-2m) and is completely covered with blooms in early summer.

Rosa 'Guinée'

This climbing hybrid tea rose is of the deepest crimson-red and appears to be almost black in some lights. It is a sturdy, vigorous grower, with plants reaching upto 15ft (5m). Sweetly perfumed, it has a flatish flower of old-world charm and blooms profusely in summer.

Salvia nemorosa 'Ostfriesland'

Plant these dark amethyst perennials in groups of at least seven to eleven plants for a persistent presence in the center of a sunny border. Growing to about 1ft (30cm) tall, they will provide a glowing wave of color from midsummer into autumn. The deep blue hidden amongst the magenta is highlighted if planted beside Lavandula angustifolia 'Hidcote'.

2 blues and mauves

No color seems to provoke so many different images as blue; it evokes the whole spectrum of emotions. For an Australian it is the color of our hills and horizons, for our whole land is clad in the blue-grey eucalyptus. It is a very positive image of beauty, water, shade, relief and repose. In Sydney there is even a blue month – November. Looking up from the harbor the natural blue haze of the native bush retreats before the intense blue of the Jacaranda tree, *Jacaranda mimosifolia*. The branches completely enclose whole suburbs in a blanket of tiny blossoms hanging in pyramidal clusters that fall to carpet houses and pavements. Walls are buried beneath cascades of blue *Plumbago auriculata* intertwined with the magenta-purple *Bougainvillea glabra* while mopheads of blue African lilies *Agapanthus africanus* stand sentinel at busy roundabouts, on verges, and driveways. November is the month before the intense heat, and the sky is blue, blue, blue. It is a blue world.

The eminent horticulturist Dr Peter Valder once described a 19th century American garden planted entirely in blue. Not only were there blue trees, shrubs and flowers, but the lady wore only ravishing *toilettes* in blue. I wondered if the lady came from a hot climate where blue gets a good press as it is often seen as a cold hard color in northern climates. For me blues are happy shades, conjuring up warm nostalgic images of childhood. Blue is never static – look for a time at the tall aconites, delphiniums, campanulas that are the stars of a blue border, there is always a feeling of movement like the light in an ever changing sky or in a restless sea. The bluebells on a woodland floor seem only a haze as we look into their depth.

Blue borders in cool climates

The color blue ranges from grey-green blue to blue with some red pigment so it becomes purple or mauve, and these were the emotional shades that I chose to take my West Green border into the sunnier beds. Blue is such an atmospheric color, so beautiful and mysterious, it reflects the elements that make up this garden. The range of blue flowers is immense: I decided on one blue border, it became two then three as I could not resist another wonderful blue thistle, a gentian, even a bright blue cabbage! The borders go through every emotion, shape and texture, housing giants and midgets of the garden world.

There are blues for every situation and scale of garden. If you have a small sunny corner that needs some drama, try a combination of blue such as *Cerinthe major* 'Purpurascens' and blue cabbage. The shapes as well as the colors of the plants provide good contrast, the round solid shape of the cabbage giving stability to the low branches of the cerinthe.

Cerinthe also needs a companion planting of a single dense color. Try it behind a group of *Lavandula angustifolia* 'Hidcote', where the lavender's intense violet flower will intensify mauve highlights in the cerinthe.

Right: Each spring I remember the hot autumn of 1992 when every bluebell was planted by hand after we mattocked the ground open

Previous page: *Iris sibirica* 'Tropic Night'

'The bluebells on a woodland floor seem only a haze as we look into their depth.'

Clear blues for spring

Spring belongs to *Brunnera macrophylla* 'Dawson's White' with cream-splashed leaves and forget-me-not blue flowers. The blue shines out under early cream flowers – the tulips *Tulipa* 'Françoise', ivory flamed with yellow, the peony style *T*. 'Mount Tacoma' and *T*. 'Maureen' which opens cream fading to white. The tulips also nod above dense clumps of *Pulmonaria* 'Roy Davidson' with its clusters of blue bells echoing watery blue sky. *Corydalis flexuosa* is a brilliant plant, easy to grow beside a dry gravel path in most climates, an intense blue flower above lacy blue-green leaves, a small necessity for an early spring border. By midsummer *Clematis* x *durandii* claims this role; although it trails it is a tidy plant, its deep indigo flowered mounds either covering spent bulbs or providing a blanket for the clear bright blue drumsticks of *Allium caeruleum* to push through.

Other early blue flowers tend to be the palest I can find such as *Veronica gentianoides* with its spikes of tiny blue flowers above a mantle of small green leaves, and *Campanula persicifolia* 'Chettle Charm', a single white flower frosted pale blue. Aquilegias seed throughout, *Aquilegia* 'Blue Bonnet' and the double pale blue *A. vulgaris* 'Blue Star' add a necessary lightness. Little clumps of the khaki green dwarf iris *I*. 'Triplicate' look smart among the blues – I love offbeat colors and look for them all the time.

Opposite: It has everything: shape, texture and wondrous color – cabbage 'Red Drumhead'

Right: *Malva sylvestris* **'Primley Blue'**

No spring garden should be without aquilegias, their delicate, iridescent heads fluttering like a cloud of butterflies above the emergent foliage of their companions. The variety is intoxicating: try *Aquilegia alpina* cultivars, the blue and white *A. caerulea* or the beautiful dark *A. vulgaris* 'Blackbird'. *Aquilegia flabellata* 'Ministar' has the brightest blue and white flowers, and as with all aquilegias their feet are clothed in leaf mounds of great beauty, branches of round scalloped leaves, welcome in their own right.

Bold summer blues

I find the bearded iris essential to carry the border towards early summer, there are so many good blues to choose from. I have planted *Iris* 'Zua' a glacial blue white, the silver-blue *I*. 'Divine Duchess', ruffled light blue and white *I*. 'Fair Dinkum' and the huge *I*. 'Sierra Grande', an absolute favorite. Further along the border is *Iris sibirica*, tall, graceful and slim with foliage that looks good all season, providing fine vertical accents after the blue flowers fade. The bright *Anchusa azurea* 'Opal' next sways beneath another sky-blue flower, *Delphinium* 'Summer Skies'. Blue and white hoods of *Aconitum* x *cammarum* 'Bicolor' follow in this patch by midsummer. The most spectacular blue *Anchusa azurea* 'Loddon Royalist' fights off the intense violet blue *Geranium* x *magnificum* that riots down the border until challenged for control by the late summer triumph *Eryngium* x *tripartitum*, a brilliant thistle that changes from green to silver blue to purple. In the driest part of the border the bright purple blues of lavender *Lavandula angustifolia* 'Hidcote' offer a frontal foil to *Cerinthe major*

'Purpurascens'. I know it's trendy, but is irresistible with its glaucous leaves an aqua-green veined with lavender, all crowned with a navy blue flower.

Every adjective is appropriate here: tall, elegant, intense, stunning, they all neatly describe the 3ft (90cm) *Iris* **'Sierra Grande' the most beautiful I think of all iris. Its standards are frozen blue white ice, its falls a midsummer blue, with ruffles as extravagant as a ballroom dancer's dress with a glimpsed underskirt of paler blue. These two tone blue iris grown in clumps will make an architectural statement of the most satisfying proportions in any garden.**

I am committed to finding more blue roses. The vigorous rambler *Rosa* 'Veilchenblau' is often called the blue rose, in fact it is not blue but its clusters of small purple-violet flowers often streaked with white are a lovely substitute. The tiny mauvey-purple buttons of the multiflora rambler *Rosa* 'Russeliana' intertwined with the small flowered *Clematis* 'Mrs Cranshaw' cover a tripod beautifully. I have placed the pinky-mauve hybrid perpetual *Rosa* 'Reine des Violettes' with the dark leaved *Penstemon digitalis* 'Husker's Red' which boasts mother of pearl flowers, a good foil for a blue bed. With some misgivings I am trying two modern roses, the large blue rose *R.* 'Charles de Gaulle' is a color triumph for a blue border and *R.* 'Dream Lover' is a centered lilac-pink. I think the flowers are a little big and too modern in shape for me but I am prepared to overlook this just to get the color.

In gentler, northern light, blue and white can be too stark a contrast, so the best trick to lift a blue border that has merged with the atmosphere by midsummer is to tuck small clumps of the common annual *Lobelia erinus* **'Cambridge Blue' into all the cracks and crevices. This very light, very pale blue seems to enhance the moody blues better than white which seems just too much of a contrast. In bright sunny light, however, we can choose whether to use white or subtler colors with blue. Creamy-yellow also lifts a blue border in cooler light so plant clumps of the yellow-eyed blue daisy** *Felicia amelloides* **among purer blues.**

The crochet blue-green leaves of *Ruta graveolens* **'Jackman's Blue' makes layers of lace leaves for a host of summer flowers to perform above. Early summer pruning keeps it to a compact mound for the bare legs of the** *Lilium regale* **'Royal Gold' or the standard rose** *R.* **'Graham Thomas' to flower on high – a perfect contrast in a warm dry garden.**

'Cerinthe. . . irresistible with its glaucous leaves an aqua green veined with lavender, all crowned with a navy blue flower.'

Right: The deservably fashionable plant *Cerinthe major* **'Purpurascens'**

Previous page: Ridged drumsticks of *Echinops ritro* **'Veitch's Blue' in the blue border looking towards the potager at West Green House**

'…blue beds
adjoin clear,
bright yellow,
leading the eye
from one
color
to the next.'

Below: The atmosphere is imbued with shades of blue at the start of the blue and yellow border at Kennerton Green

Opposite: *Echinops ritro* **'Veitch's Blue' – geometric balls of blue spikes**

Blues in warmer climates

Blue is used differently in my Australian garden, largely in blocks to tie other colors together. At Kennerton Green sky blue beds adjoin clear bright yellow, leading the eye from one color to the next. Under a hot sky these colors are clean and bright even on the hottest days, while in cooler climates brilliant yellow needs subduing, it makes a lovely accompaniment to navy blue. I love blue spiky plants pushing up through green foliage and include the Canterbury bells, *Campanula medium*, among my all-time favorites. I have planted these along with clumps of blue cupped *Campanula persicifolia* and the stiff steel blue drumsticks of powdery blue *Echinops ritro* 'Veitch's Blue' behind banks of *Centaurea montana*, a most hardy plant.

Echinops need space and would overpower a small garden but if you fall in love with the thistle flowers try growing eryngium for the same effect. *Eryngium* 'Miss Wilmott's Ghost' will grow to about 3ft (1m) but spread no more than 1ft (30cm), producing silvery blue flowers. Or try *E.* x *tripartitum* which changes from green to silver to purple-blue.

Perovskia 'Blue Spire' is a good plant for dry patches, with tall lavender-blue spikes, and monkshood *Aconitum napellus* likes the shade. I use *Allium giganteum*, tall stems with giant purple balls, to usher in a patch of bluey-mauve where treasured *Rhododendron* 'Blue Diamond' back into a cool corner. The Swan River daisy *Brachyscombe iberidifolia* accompanies the annual *Viola* 'Moody Blue', and the purple wallflower *Erysimum*

'Bowles' Mauve' flowers from winter's end till midsummer. The common foxglove *Digitalis purpurea* saturates the end of my blue border in a haze of mauve which turns back to blue with drifts of *Iris* 'China Blue' rising through *Lithospermum diffusum*, a ground hugging blue flower that responds to the driest conditions.

This blue bed then turns again to yellow, then back to the blue theme where an avenue of five large *Ceanothus* 'Blue Pacific' form huge balls of intense blue flowers in spring, perfect with the background blue of Dutch Iris, rising through the Japanese woodland plant *Epimedium*, its flowers the softest yellow. The ceanothus are surrounded by clipped balls of *Lavandula angustifolia* or *L. x allardii*, a firm favorite in Australian gardens, and blue flowers carry the story through to midsummer. Blocks of yellow and blue continue for 110yds (100m) before meeting an embankment of white to adjust the eye to the next story.

Ceanothus are much too beautiful to dismiss but I have found that, for no reason at all, they can die suddenly leaving huge gaps. *Ceanothus* 'Gloire de Versailles', with masses of powder blue flowers to match the cool blue skies of the early season, is at home given space and underplanted with pale blues and creams, but equally happy in confined spaces trained against a greyish or honey-colored wall or fence. Or place the denser purple-blue *C.* 'Concha' against a wall for a late spring show. Lavenders are also irresistible but they too can depart suddenly, generally from too much moisture on a rich soil.

blue favorites

Aconitum 'Spark's Variety'

Like late summer fine delphiniums, they are tall spires of hooded flowers up to 4ft (1.2m) tall. This variety includes all the somber dark blue shades that suggest the far recesses of a cloister, its hidden face providing a sense of mystery. Plants come in white and shades of blue and will flower in semi-shade or full sun in rich soil.

Anchusa azurea 'Loddon Royalist'

Although a perennial, I find in England I must treat it as an annual. Incredibly intense bright blue flowers that grow to 4ft (1.2m) on hairy stems. It is the most marvellous blue perennial I've seen, flowering from mid-spring to summer.

Campanula persicifolia 'Chettle Charm'

Has fine but strong stems up to 3ft (1m) tall, with bell-shaped flowers just tinged with blue. This perennial likes full sun and a good soil and should be grown in groups of five to seven plants to create an effect.

Cerinthe major 'Purpurascens'

I can never decide whether cerinthe or alliums are the wonder plants of today. Cerinthe is an irresistible addition, with glaucous blue-green foliage and navy blue flowers all summer. It is a bushy plant, about 2ft (60cm) tall, and is at its best when grown in generous clumps in mid-border. It thrives in full sun but will tolerate partial shade. Treat it as an annual in most cool, temperate climates, but in warmer areas you can cut it back and it will return.

Ceanothus 'Blue Pacific'

A tall, broad shrub that can grow to 6ft (2m), covered by masses of dense, intense, bright blue flowers in spring. It needs well-drained soil and an open position, and can be trained against walls. Unfortunately ceanothus tend to be shortlived but replacements grow quickly.

Clematis 'Perle d'Azur'

A beautiful, misty, pale blue-flowered climber that can go to 15ft (5m) in a mass of midsummer blooms. Clematis do not like to have their roots disturbed and in warmer areas a below-surface rock placed over their roots keeps them cool. I have allowed this clematis to grow alongside *Rosa* 'Veilchenblau'. I do like this combination.

Delphinium 'Pacific Giant'

Tall spikes of blue flowers up to 6ft (2m), that come in all shades of blue from near-white mauve to blue-black. Snails and slugs feast on their new shoots, but they are the superstars of any summer border. They are also the heart-breakers of a blue border if they are not well staked, for the stems are brittle and easily snapped in wind and rain.

Jacaranda mimosifolia

Although the tender jacaranda is not suitable for northern European gardens, this tall tree is a wonderful addition to any sub-tropical or frost-free Mediterranean climate garden. Covered with ferny, mid-green foliage, for three weeks in summer it is covered by large clusters of bell-shaped flowers of jacaranda-blue in large clusters. It will cope with some frost but must be covered as a small plant in frosty areas. It tends to be a 'dirty' tree in cooler districts where it will lose its foliage.

Rosa 'Veilchenblau'

A rambling rose that sends out bunches of tiny flowers of a blue-lilac color, semi-double with a white eye. It is fragrant and vigorous growing to nearly 15ft (5m) feet. Although said to fade in the sun, I have not found this.

Syringa vulgaris (lilac)

One Sunday morning in Denmark I saw a pastor in black vestments on the steps of a white church, the entire scene surrounded by a lilac hedge in full flower. This memory is one of my most treasured mind pictures. Lilacs are large bushes that can grow to 15ft (5m) tall and varieties are available in pinks, purples, lavenders, creams and white – flowering in mid-spring with a heady perfume.

Opposite: *Delphinium* **'Black Night'**

'mauve . . . glows on dull days, is silvery under raindrops and has a luminosity I have never seen in the southern hemisphere.'

Moody mauves

In cool temperate gardens in North America, Ireland and Britain, mauve seems to shine. It glows on dull days, is silvery under raindrops and has a luminosity I have never seen in the southern hemisphere. On hot afternoons under brilliant sky mauve needs to be backed with stronger shades. Unlike lavender, it seems to bleach under intense sunlight, but when backed by blue to keep it cool mauve is strong enough to hold its own.

Dusty mauve also strengthens when backed by leaves of steel grey or polished ebony. The dark Shiraz leaves of *Geranium traversii* var. *elegans* 'Crûg Strain' forms neat spreading mounds, its small white flower, smudged with pink, takes on the mauve shades of its neighbors. While the leaves create all the theater that mauve requires.

Yellow and mauve are very fashionable but they are not two colors I like together unless there are masses of blues to divide them. Though there is a surprise element from the clash of contrary colors, I find it worrying – but this is the joy of gardening. I have taken as my motto the one inscribed over the door in the 1720s at West Green House that reads 'Do as you please'. Knowing what is said of General Hawley's character it probably actually refers to rather dubious activities but I am happy to interpret it as offering carte blanche to keen gardeners!

Raindrops enhance the shades of mauve in *Iris germanica* 'Gallant Rogue' and double blue aquilegia in the garden of West Green House

'…a metallic conductor that flows from the neighboring bed of rich jewel colors through to the gentler world of mauve, lilac and pink.'

Opposite above: *Allium cristophii* (fore-ground) are the mauve balls of stars under the old apple tree in the walled garden

Opposite below: Clumps of the bright purple *Allium giganteum* are repeated through-out the garden at West Green House

Left: *Iris germanica* 'Twice Delightful' fills the June gap in an English summer border

Dappled mauves in warm climates

While mauves have their own borders in my English garden, I haven't given them such a major role under the hot Australian sun: at Kennerton Green they make their appearance under the dappled light of my cherry tree lined bulb walk. This is the antithesis of a formal bulb walk such as the one so admired at Sissinghurst – a haphazard group of bulbs and plants that commences flowering with spring's thimble-sized mauve crocus and concludes with the faded mauve-grey *Hosta* 'Hadspen Blue' sheltering beneath the trees as the mercury soars.

I wanted the eye to travel through my cherry trees to the garden's 'showstopper' at one end of the walk, the giant parasol of *Wisteria sinensis*. Trained over the years to form a huge perfumed umbrella, this is host to the hum of a thousand bees, and its petals create a lavender carpet beneath. I did not want to plant bluebells in this bulb walk, nor daffodils and narcissus in the garden beds. I think they are like some house-guests – they give great joy at the time but take for ever to tidy up after!

When planting under blossoming trees, think of the color of the canopy as well as the colors in the carpet you are fabricating. For example, the mauves, lilacs and blues that follow pink on the color wheel are complementary shades, but these colors are also energetic enough to tell a story in their own right, so bulbs in these shades are ideal for planting where the light is sifted through pink blossom on high.

My bulb planting is intended to be a mixture of tones enhanced by the light reflected through oceans of pink blossom above. I first formed a dense ground-hugging mat in lavender-blue and white with huge purple violets *Viola odorata*, their clumps as old as the garden. I added sweetly smelling traditional cream freesias along with a splashy new blue hybrid, and primroses, both the small shy ones of childhood and the big bold hybrid white and blue polyanthus – attacked daily by voracious bower-birds who have shifted their fascination for Sydney's blue milk-bottle tops to my garden. The glossy bronze leaves and deep blue flowers of *Ajuga reptans* 'Jungle Beauty' trail everywhere, and I pray that the once prominent foam flower *Tiarella cordifolia* will return, its cream feathery flowers so beautiful in deep shade, but it scorches if trapped in the sun.

The tiny double white flowers of *Arabis subsp. caucasica* 'Flora Pleno' surround clumps of *Ornithogalum nutans* with strictly marked green and white leaves and silver-white flowers creating one huge pale floor-covering beneath the large pink and white blossom heads. Through this the mauves and lavenders peer, there are tulips, tulips and more tulips in every shade of lavender, mauve and white I can find, forming a swinging curve that takes the eye through the trees and beyond. Plantings of the deep purple *Tulipa* 'Queen of Night' add depth to the mauve-blue ruffles of *T.* 'Blue Parrot'. The Tyrian *T.* 'Negrita' is a powerful purple color that makes me shudder, and it is planted here along with the oversized double-white *T.* 'White Parrot' which prevents the purple

and mauve shades of more tulips – *T.* 'Blue Beauty', *T.* 'Atilla' and *T.* 'Purple Prince' – from becoming monotonous.

The ground hugging species tulips are often overlooked in favor of more flamboyant varieties but in spring they neatly and precisely carpet beds with their tiny flowers. Try *Tulipa bakeri* 'Lilac Wonder' crammed into wide saucer pots or window boxes – a delight on city terraces where tar and cement forget to remind that spring has come.

Dutch iris, not named varieties but a good mix of blues, purples and whites from our bulb-grower, take over as tulips fade through the plague of encroaching forget-me-nots which is so atmospheric for a few weeks. The final touch is a few clumps of bearded iris, retrieved from a planting disaster: I purchased what I thought was a number of very pale blue irises for another part of the garden, on flowering they were stitched with the strongest purple-blue possible, garish in strong light. My Presbyterian blood saved them from the rubbish tip and I interred them in the deepest shade of Cherry Walk. What a wonderful thing light is, in dappled shade their purplish-mauves glow and turn quite respectable, and I'm really quite fond of them now.

A passion for shades of blue includes the blue *Clematis* 'Perle d'Azur' scrambling up a tripod to the navy hoods of *Aconitum* 'Spark's Variety' interwoven with the self-seeding pale blue annual *Nigella damascena*

Blue and mauve annual patterns

In Mittagong my garden must look beautiful very early in the spring as it opens to thousands of visitors on behalf of the local charity Tulip Festival. Originally the view across the entrance bed was spoiled by a very utilitarian-looking garage, so we brought in loads of soil and made a mini mountain with three terraces. On the top level I planted a large group of the large azalea 'Alba Magna' to make it look like Mount Fuji in spring. The second terrace had been intended for perennials but the drainage was too severe for them so it is now a grey foliage border. The bottom border had to be particularly beautiful as that is where the eye first falls. This meant it had to be planted with annuals.

To ensure there would be structure even when annuals are tiring, I planted box *Buxus sempervirens* in a zigzag design. In keeping with nearby planting I have made zigzags of blues and white, generally using blue violas with white antirrhinums. Some years I use a pale blue viola, others a deep blue, and sometimes a mixture available in Australia called 'Moody Blues'. This bed is echoed around the corner – where it is much drier and sunnier – in a permanent zigzag bed filled with low growing lavender and rosemary, overhung with the pink rambling rose *Rosa* 'Albertine'.

Box cut into zigzag shapes or scallops and filled with annuals is a most unusual and eye catching treatment for any bed large or small. Or use a grey-leaved edging plant such as santolina or dwarf lavender, both of which are particularly effective when infilled with whites and pale blues.

mauve favorites

Allium cristophii

A stunning addition to any garden, in early summer large flower-heads of silver-lilac balls made up of tiny star-like flowers appear, lighting up any border with their metallic glint. They grow to about 1ft (30cm) and flourish in semi-shade and full sun in well-drained soils. Leave some unpicked where they will dry *in situ* to a silver fawn, lasting right through autumn.

Erysimum 'Bowles' Mauve'

A perennial wallflower that is covered with small shaded mauve flat flowers above greyish foliage. In warmer areas, it flowers from late winter until midsummer spreading an understudy of stiff stems – excellent supports for later growing plants. It is shortlived in cooler temperate areas and must be replaced from cuttings. It likes full sun and grows to 20in (50cm). A must for early season color.

Lavandula stoechas

French lavender forms a compact perennial grey-green bush about 30in (75cm) tall with dense ovoid spikes of dark purple flowers with clusters of pinkish-purple bracts on top. Sun-loving, it flowers all summer in well-drained gravelly soil, but is not reliably hardy in cold gardens.

Opposite: The precision cut hedges of box that trap spring flowering annuals at Kennerton Green illustrate the importance of structure in a garden in maintaining design after the flowers are spent

Right: The intense blue of *Centaurea montana* – a hardy long-flowering perennial

Papaver orientale 'Patty's Plum'

This delicious perennial poppy emerges in early spring with clusters of hairy green leaves followed by fat buds like crunched-up crêpe paper, opening in early summer to form huge mauve and dusky plum flowers on stems about 4ft (1.25m) tall. It will flower in semi-shade or in sun in well fertilized and drained soil. It spreads across the bed, so when flowering is finished and the plant cut back, it leaves a large empty space so its a good idea to plant it towards the back of the border although its ferny leaf quickly reappears.

Penstemon 'Sour Grapes'

Australian nurseryman David Glen describes this increasingly popular penstemon as 'soft green, amethyst and blue flowers like unripe grapes'. Penstemons resemble smaller growing foxgloves with bell-shaped flowers hanging down strong stems. A perennial in cool temperate climates, they are said to be able to withstand frost as long as the roots are not waterlogged, but I treat them as an annual.

Rosa 'William Lobb'

This vigorous Moss rose grows to 6ft (2m) tall, its arching stems best supported on a tripod. 'Mossy' buds open to fully double cupped highly scented flowers of magenta-purple fading to a dusky violet. All roses need sun, well manured soil and plenty of water.

Tulipa 'Blue Parrot'

A large luscious tulip on a strong stem with extravagant frilled petals in harmonious shades of lavender, blue and purple. Planted in warmer climates it will flower in part shade or full sun. In cooler areas, plant in full sun. Bulbs should be lifted after the leaves have turned brown.

Tricyrtis formosana

The toad lily produces spikes of white orchid-shaped flowers heavily spotted with pinkish-purple above shiny dark, varied leaves which are also often dotted with purple. This exotic perennial grows to about 3ft (90cm) and looks as if it should be in an equatorial jungle but it will grow in rich moist soil in sun or semi-shade. Provide it with a deep winter mulch in cooler areas.

3 | whites

Clear classic white looks beautiful, I feel, in a garden with clear strong light such as my Australian garden, but in England I find it can be too harsh on its own. It needs to be backed by the equally strong green of hedges and trees, or placed against grey walls or on trellises painted in sage green or grey. It is also elegant against brick walls where there is major planting of solid green. It is a case of an equal mixing of color strengths, for mellow colors and lights seem to respond to half tones. Duller whites are easier to place in soft light, right against bricks slightly filmed in moss or stained with leaching lime.

White under cool skies

I had thought that during the two years we were reclaiming the West Green garden, I had come to understand its light and atmosphere, but I was wrong. The first season I cheerfully planted white plants inside the walled garden. As they flowered that first spring they looked too new, too modern for the age and ambience inherent to an old walled garden. After some seasons of tinkering, I have now barrowed most of the plants away and with spring approaching I am anxious to judge how my theories on aged white survive.

The garden will still be white but included are parchment whites, whites washed with a suggestion of pink, veined in plum and burgundy, whites with deep eyes and splashes. The tripods now await the sturdy trails of the dainty single climbing rose, *Rosa* 'Francis E. Lester', large clusters of white flowers just edged with pink, a compliant plant that will be as happy at West Green House as it is around the lake in my Australian garden.

The torn-fringed *R.* 'Frimbiata' has also come with me, it's such an unusual rose with its fringed edge and white flat face flecked with pink. A good find has been the barely white modern English shrub rose *R.* 'Jacqueline du Pré', wide faced with golden stamens. Another rose in these tones is *R.* 'Sally Holmes', joining a splash of true white in a group of the English rose, *R.* 'Winchester Cathedral'. A tiny Japanese rose *R.* 'Nozomi', a miniature white and pearl pink, is looped over canes and curves 8in (20cm) high to scollop both sides of the border.

Grey foliage is useful to soften white. By midsummer in cooler climates the soft white tufts of *Anaphalis triplinervis* smother the lower branches of tall grey-green globe artichokes that support the gooseneck white flowers of *Lysimachia clethroides*. In a smaller space combine silver and grey leaved herbs such as santolina or lavenders with stark whites, underplant white roses or edge a white bed with the soft silvery lamb's ears of *Stachys byzantina*.

The crêpe paper flowers of the oriental poppy *Papaver* 'Black and White' have a central dark blotch like tea leaves left in the bottom of a teacup, and not quite snow white petals; they will rise behind the silvery soft furry leaves of *Stachys byzantina*. Both the pure white, and pink and white varieties of the tall 5ft (1.5m) annual *Cleome* will wave through the spent roses along with the single white cosmos, equally tall above its foaming foliage. Glamorous Asiatic Lilies,

include *Lilium* 'Mont Blanc', white with deep pink tipped stamens, and 'Sterling Star', pinpoints of burgundy on white will join the Turk's caps *L. martagon* var. *album* and whitish tiger lilies.

Clouds of ethereal white *Crambe cordifolia* and *Gypsophila* will provide a bridal veil to break up dense white spires of *Campanula persicifolia alba*, *Digitalis alba*, and the tall swords of *Delphinium* 'Galahad'. *Gaura lindheimeri* proffers clouds of whitish pink butterfly flowers that will hide the leaves of *Iris germanica* 'Palamino', its flowers shell pink with white faces, whose beauty is echoed by the peony *P.* 'Miss America' in June. Gossamer flower clouds, watercolor washes across petals, and grey leaves will create old white, a gentle white for the soft light captured within the garden's tall walls.

I would love to conclude a white garden with a small tree its leaves so variegated they are nearly white falling from horizontal branches tiered to resemble a royal wedding cake. *Cornus controversa* 'Variegata' in full flower is a romatic image, a white veil of flowers, a happy ever after ending to a bed of white. They grow in cool climate gardens in Australia, but in cooler areas they appreciate a sheltered corner away from cold winds.

White alstroemeria in front of hastily planted white *Antirrhinum* – a garden saviour after a wet winter had drowned two groups of *Lavandula angustifolia* 'Alba'

Previous page: The incandescent whiteness of *Lilium* 'Casa Blanca'

'It is a case
of an equal
mixing of color
strengths, for
mellow colors and
lights seem to
respond to half
tones.'

'. . . it is dazzling to look down on the interplay of shape, size and textures of the white on white. . .'

Cool white borders for warm climates

For as long as I can remember the cottage has been framed in a snow white lace ruff of intricately planted annuals, a seasonally changing design that can include white tulips, fragrant stocks, annual iberis and ranunculi, all edged with white violas cushioned between great balls of *Iberis sempervirens*. Although white is not an easy color for many dry countries, I am fortunate that my garden is far from the red plains where whites can turn so dusty and muddy. I have not tampered with the garden's tradition that, as spring ends, the display is changed to 'Vanilla' marigolds and white nicotiana, zinnias and antirrhinums, sometimes interwoven with the fine foliage of cosmos – a simple summer collection under garlands of the whiteish rambling rose *Rosa* 'Wedding Day'. Somehow stray white delphiniums and *Nicotiana sylvestris* have settled themselves at the back of the bed, along with the resident tree peonies.

Fashion has swung against Kennerton Green's white borders of predominantly cottage garden annuals, a remnant of elegant Edwardian style. But it is dazzling to look down on the interplay of shape, size and textures of the white on white, thousands of tiny flowers, slivers of white ice planted under a cool sun in early spring. It's breathtaking, and I hope it may awaken an interest in a dismissed range of flowers that bloom long before the summer herbaceous border – today's fashion statement – even considers taking the floor.

The simplicity of the white flowers echoes the spirit of the house. The plants are as unpretentious as the house itself, an innocent picture strayed from the pages of a Kate Greenaway illustration.

Every autumn David McKinlay and I plan, and David plants, our ribbons of annuals. For your own white border try *Iberis sempervirens* with annual *Viola*, *Lobularia maritima* and *Alyssum* at the front; annual *Ranunculus* 'Rembrandt' selection with *Matthiola incana*, annual *iberis* and *Antirrhinum majus* in the middle and at the back perennial delphinuium hybrids with annual *Nicotiana sylvestris*. In a small garden for high summer try low growing white marigolds, nicotiana, white zinnias, antirrhinums, and white annual salvia – all are good in beds but equally for attractive summer displays in troughs and tubs.

In the bed to the east of the house the white flowers are repeated under the budding spring trees like a small frill of lace on an expensive petticoat. By summer this lacy river is overtaken by a line of spreading oak-leaved *Hydrangea quercifolia*, its long clusters of white flowers repeating the white theme, covering the recently emptied bed to meet the green cushions of the trimmed *Iberis sempervirens*. It provides a spot of pure white in what has otherwise become cavernous blue-green shade.

The main perennial inhabitants of this bed are rhododendrons. The older ones are all shades of pink but those I have planted are mostly creams and white. One of my favorite shrubs is *Rhododendron* 'Frangrantissimum', its large white trumpet shaped flowers smelling of nutmeg. It is among the last of the rhododendrons to flower in spring and I plant it again and again to follow the white starry flowers of the beautiful *Magnolia stellata*, small trees planted in groups so their flowers form a dense constellation. The white borders run into a curve of green flowers, which shine out of the deep Australian summer shade.

White with pink

I am an addict for glossy garden books, I devour the latest trends, sigh over stunning combinations and mentally barrow my garden away before I have reached the final page. Occasionally the pictures of one garden become a more permanent ideal, referred to over and over again. Mrs William S. Paley's garden on Long Island near New York City was one such inspiration, a photograph showing what looked like a circular sloping bank massed in pink and white *Cornus* (dogwoods), its floor a thicket of azaleas stopping abruptly by a simple circular pool. One winter's afternoon when I was burning the autumn rubbish down beyond the old Kennerton Green vegetable plot, alongside the old buildings and the leaky dam, my mind began gradually to see that American garden taking place there. Such a vision of pink and white around a basin of water may be colonial in origin, but large plantings of a limited range of plants in a controlled palette ensure the simplicity of style that is so suitable for my country garden.

A year later a giant machine arrived to clear the dam and make a perfect oval lake, its banks to be sown to grass, the surrounds gently sloped. The plan was to capture a little of the effect of my American image, but of course the new lake filled and emptied immediately, so the machine had to return to remake it; the beautifully graded slope was pure compacted clay, and the northern end of the garden was so exposed to ferocious winds that many of my early plants died. With hindsight we should have removed all the clay from the top, but I trembled to touch the banks, so the trees and shrubs were planted by digging huge holes in the clay and filling them with compost and manure. I planted masses of the American dogwood, but the hot winds soon thinned their ranks. *Cornus florida* is the hardiest in a dryish climate, but even when regularly watered it becomes very stressed by late summer while *Cornus kousa* has flourished – I suspect its position allows it to capture more moisture. Azaleas and rhododendrons were similarly drought-susceptible so my American dream had to be adapted to Australian reality.

The desired pink canopy was achieved with the earliest flowering crab apple *Malus floribunda*, a mass of deep pink buds opening to the palest pink. *Davidia involucrata* initially struggled but has survived, its delicate flowers resemble a washing line of white handkerchiefs. All types of *Deutzia* enjoy the climate, and cushions of star-white flowers of *Deutzia crenata* var. *nakaiana* 'Nikko' are excellent in the front of a border.

Spring awakens the double flowered white lilac *Syringa vulgaris* 'Madame Lemoine', which forms a heavy mass beside the white firework-like flowers of *Cytisus* x *praecox* 'Albus'. The immense green-white flowers of *Viburnum macrocephalum* are spectacular snowballs for spring and *Hydrangea paniculata* 'Grandiflora' produces wonderful summer mounds of large white pyramidal flowers. *Viburnum opulus* 'Notcutt's Variety' has dense white flowers which are replaced by red berries in early autumn.

The tissue paper flowers of Helianthemum 'The Bride' love sun and dry feet, a small spreading plant that makes a companionable ground cover of thousands of single gold-centered white blooms above leaves of dusty green.

Opposite: Old pink azaleas and aquilegia burst into flower before the white ribbon border begins to flower in spring

Below: The elegant *Viburnum plicatum* 'Mariesii' balances white flowers along horizontal stems

A rose garden

Roses have replaced many more tender plants at Kennerton Green. Lax uncontrolled bush roses now provide clouds of pink and white in early summer – rather than my planned dogwood blossoms. There is only one David Austin rose that likes me, and the flowers of *Rosa* 'Constance Spry' are perfect for this garden, like cups of pink sugar. Another 'pink pink' is *R.* 'Königin von Dänemark', a quartered Alba rose which I have planted in clumps of threes or fives interspersed with the heavily scented dropping pink heads of the Centifolia rose *Rosa* 'Fantin-Latour'. The modern spreading shrub rose *R.* 'Raubritter' fights the winds along the edge with the small flowered fringed Rugosas *R.* 'Fimbriata' and *R.* 'Grootendorst', their petals looking as if they have been cut by pinking shears.

This part of the garden is a cheerful candyfloss palette, but it initially lacked drama. This is now supplied by a carpet of old pinks *Dianthus allwoodii* – I lifted a clump from the original garden, and it multiplied swiftly to form a plush covering of shocking pink, bleached here and there by *Cerastium tomentosum*, *Alyssum saxatile* and pure white verbena. Around the lake I planted a mixture of pink and white climbers and ramblers but these were a straggly mistake and now they are being replaced by the sturdy rambler *Rosa* 'Francis E. Lester'. The huge blossoms of *R.* 'Madame Grégoire Staechelin' sporadically weave through it to ensure the planting isn't too polite.

The steep bank into the lake was planned as a wall of bearded irises meeting a pale pink

Louisiana iris at the water's edge. The first year the soft ruffles of five hundred *Iris* 'Beverly Sills' were planted it was sensational, but by season's end it was a horrible sight as they were choked beneath sorrel *Rumex acetosa* which defied all recommended forms of eradication. The iris have since been removed and for now we rotate annuals, hoping the constant re-digging and spraying will allow us to replant eventually.

Pink and white roses have their own garden at Kennerton Green, surrounding a small expanse of water. A narrow path leads to 6ft (2m) high hedges of *Cupressus torulosa*. Yew is very difficult to grow in the cooler climates of the southern hemisphere but well clipped Cypressus makes a good substitute. The hedge opens to reveal an oblong garden with a central long narrow pond reflects predominantly pink and white standard roses on either side. On either side parallel iron arches support the modern floribunda climber *Rosa* 'Iceberg' which shades secluded seats. At the far end a partly shaded shepherdess rises above a cool cream white *Rosa* 'Valerie Swane' which I planted to commemorate the life of a friend and gardener.

The garden was originally planted by Lady Pagan with beautiful cream, pink and white hybrid teas and floribundas that the catalogues of two decades ago could supply. My mother also loved this style of rose so the garden is a mixture of their choices: the white hybrid teas *Rosa* 'Virgo' and *R.* 'Silver Jubilee', the pink *R.* 'Elizabeth Harkness', the fragrant pink-edged cream of *R.* 'Princesse de Monaco', pink tinged creamy-yellow *R.* 'Peace', pale pink *R.* 'Pink Parfait', the small white centered

pale pink flowers of *R.* 'Ballerina' and the greatest pink of all, *R.* 'Queen Elizabeth', a superb floribunda. New plantings have included *R.* 'Margaret Merril', a white floribunda with a satin pink finish; *R.* 'Seduction' a large rose of cream, its edges frills of the palest pink; the champagne roses *R.* 'Vanilla' and *R.* 'Champagne', and the pale pink to white Irish rose *R.* 'Souvenir de Saint Anne's', a semi-single sport of *R.* 'Souvenir de la Malmaison'.

There are rose types that can be slotted into any garden so even a small space can be transformed into a sensuous rose garden providing it gets enough sun. Choose from climbers reaching at least 16ft (5m), tall standards at 8ft (2.5m), half standards at 6ft (2m), bush roses from 3-6ft (1-2m) and ground hugging roses such as the generous pink *Rosa* 'Raubritter'.

Some of the most delightful are:

Rosa 'Fantin-Latour'

A tall, sturdy shrub rose growing up to 6ft (2m). This Centifolia rose flowers as a shell pink cup bursting with slightly deeper pink petals in summer. Roses like to be well fed with manure, and also like rose food in early spring. This rose reappears in every garden I grow.

Rosa 'Francis E. Lester'

Like the rose *R.* 'Wedding Day' (*see p.69*), this rambler is another trademark. It is a strong, well-leaved rose growing to 15ft (5m) in clusters of fragrant, single white flowers in midsummer, their edges touched with pink. Although (like all roses), it likes to be fed, it will still perform in dry soil.

Rosa 'Königin Von Dänemark'

This is the essence of an old rose, or Alba rose, in the softest pink with a grey-green foliage growing to 4ft (1.2m). The flowers are perfumed and large, its petals arranged in quarters.

Rosa 'Madeleine Selzer'

The double ice-lemon blooms of this rambling, but not too vigorous, rose appear only once a year, with attractive light green leaves. I have several which seem as happy growing in a gravel path as in good soil.

Opposite: An old pink rose found by an abandoned cottage now rises above *Dianthus allwoodii* in Mittagong

Left: The floribunda *Rosa* 'Saint John'

'. . . a Regency fantasy that seems to float on the waterline.'

The fashion conscious of the garden world favor heritage roses today and question this type of planting, but I love it for it represents the evolution of a garden and respect for past gardeners. The high hedges of my pink and white garden contain their own sensuous world: there are roses standing erect on grafted stems and shrub roses clutching at passing skirts, roses tumbling from arches and cascading from knarled weeping standards.

It is especially important in smaller gardens to use space effectively, with a careful choice of plants for underplanting. Roses will grow beautifully in dry climates so it is easy to forget that they need lots of nourishment and water to give their best, and underplanting must take this into account. Good low level companions for roses are *Nepeta* (catmint) and lavenders as they don't need too much water. However, these choices can become rampant and difficult to maintain, and bulbs and annuals can be a better solution. Standard roses look particularly bare in early spring but can be brought to life by underplanting with almost any bulb, the white fringed *Tulipa* 'Swan Wings' or the bells of *Allium triquetrum* could both be considered.

The hedges not only create a private world, and shield humans and roses from winds, they also capture clear light, ensuring the colors remain true and clear, less subtle than when confined amongst other plants in a herbaceous border. The underplanting of pink forget-me-nots, arabis and tulips reflects this gaiety. It would be difficult to capture

similar sensations in larger rose gardens, but the confining hedges are a double-edged sword for humidity collects and stays among the glorious abundance, and the dreaded black spot takes hold by late spring.

Pink and white planting can sometimes look far too dainty so give white and pink roses an injection of exuberance by adding a few bold stripes such as those of the hybrid perpetual roses R. 'Ferdinand Pichard', with its brilliant stripes of crimson on soft pink, or the stylish R. 'Baron Girod de l'Ain' – its deep cups of crimson are edged with a white thread.

White trees with colors underfoot

I think it was the words of the 23rd Psalm 'He maketh me to lie down in green pastures, he leadeth me beside still waters, he restoreth my soul' that led me to plant a grove of white trees beside deep dark water. My Mother died at Kennerton Green in July 1991 as we were discussing a new area to plant. We both liked the idea of white birch trees and a woodland garden – my mother's last words were a request for an archway to enter this garden. Today the archway is a long cage of two parallel compartments filled with white doves, leading to a grove of three hundred slim white-trunked birch trees, a Betula Moss's selection, their lacy twigs holding tiny leaves that shimmer and talk to each other in the wind. It is a peaceful place enclosing a pond, now filled with Louisiana iris in blue and white, with white waterlilies surrounding a Chinoiserie birdcage, a Regency fantasy that seems to float on the waterline.

The pond with its surrounding bluebell woodland was made to mark the life of my mother, Una Abbott.

Previous page: Enclosed in tall hedges of *Cypressus torulosa*, a shepherdess guards the rose garden at Kennerton Green in early November.

The woodland floor is an ever changing carpet of small bulbs. Early crocus, *Crocus chrysanthus* in soft pale blue, are followed by the nodding yellow bonnets of the hoop petticoat daffodil, *Narcissus bulbocodium*, tiny blooms naturalising at an extraordinary rate. Their faces are soon covered by thousands of blue scillas (Spanish bluebells); these were all planted by hand, mainly using a crowbar to make cracks in the earth when autumn rains were late. Beside the bluebells large patches of aromatic old-fashioned creamy white *Freesia refracta* var. *alba* add a beautiful perfume that is very special. I am fortunate to live in a warm enough climate in Australia to be able to naturalize freesias, however we do have light frosts and freesias tend every second or third year only to flower in sheltered pockets, while the hoop petticoats will flower under the most extreme conditions. The bulbs form a charming progressive tapestry of blue, yellow, blue and white, before the spikes of tall white foxglove *Digitalis alba* flower in early summer to rival the white birch trunks. Later in the year the autumn crocus (known as the autumn daffodil in England) *Sternbergia lutea* shines out a brilliant yellow among the small autumn leaves.

While freesias are not an option in northern climates, other bulbs provide a similar light touch. Nodding fritillaries and dainty *Narcissus* bring spots of light to a garden in early spring after the welcome primroses.

A woodland is not just a flat space, but an area of gullies, mounds and small embankments, so this birch grove is shaped with hillocks, a mini range of hills, each higher than the last, covered by the tapestry of flowers. A bank behind the pond is planted with the rugosa rose *Rosa* 'Schneezwerg', white with yellow stamens; crevices in walls host *Iberis sempervirens*, the heady clove-perfumed *Dianthus* 'Mrs Sinkins', and *Cerastium tomentosum*, a mat forming ground cover that deserves its common name of 'snow in summer'.

I often sit on the bench beside the pond and reflect on this foolhardy enterprise, for although birches will grow in well tended beds in our climate, they are not ideal for woodland plantings at Mittagong. But all gardeners have dreams of the beauty they wish to create: for me it was an intermingling of white trees, tall white flowers and a carpet of blue, white and yellow, a softening of roses and an entrance through clouds of white *Spiraea* 'Arguta' in spring with its tiniest of light green leaves, its flowers a bridal veil.

If a garden is an expression of paradise, these plans are my idea of a paradise garden. It is a garden of white trees, a minimalist approach, a simplistic use of blocks of one plant, three hundred birch trees, the floor in bold blocks of blue, white and yellow. At West Green we are also planting birch trees, *Betula jacquemontii*, as a backdrop to stiff graded hedges of dark green yew, a transition of lightness where woodland meets classical formality.

white favorites

Cleome hassleriana

This spider flower is a strong-stemmed annual that grows in full sun to 4-5ft (1.5m) tall, flowering in midsummer. Varieties come in white, light magenta or pink with spider-like petals that appear at the top of the stem.

Crambe cordifolia

Tiny scented gypsophila-like flowers cloud in clusters from 6ft (2m) tall strong stems, above a clump of large mid-green leaves. The dainty flowers appear from late spring through midsummer. *Crambe cordifolia* needs a sunny position and will tolerate dry soils but I have had difficulty establishing it in cool temperate climates.

Iberis sempervirens

Candytuft is a groundcovering perennial covered with tiny white flowers in spring, in sun or semi-shade. Old plants will develop into mounds that can be trained to hang over terraces. If candytuft is clipped after flowering, it provides a pleasing green shape all summer. There is also a sun-loving annual iberis with similar flowers but growing to around 9in (20cm) tall.

Lysimachia clethroides

In mid and late summer tall, light stems of loosestrife will soften any border. It grows to about 3ft (1m) with slender stems which curl over then straighten up slightly like goose's necks, topped with clusters of tiny white flowers. Loosestrife will grow in semi-shade or sun but prefers a reasonably moist soil.

Matthiola incana

This stock is a sweetly-smelling annual with fat spikes around 8-10in (20-25cm) tall, covered by double rosettes of flowers. It likes a well-mulched bed and flowers for around six weeks in late spring or early summer. Available in shades of lavender, pink and white. I only use white.

Ornithogalum nutans

This spring bulb has white star-like flowers with a distinctive green line. Plants grow to around 8in (20cm), often in shady patches, and they naturalize well. I like to use them to underplant tulips.

Rosa 'Wedding Day'

This rambling rose has grown and flowered for me in the subtropics, in Mediterranean and in cool temperate climate zones. Soft apricot buds open to clusters of single cream, then white fragrant flowers. In five years, these plants have grown so vigorously that two-thirds of the house at Kennerton Green is now swagged with 'Wedding Day'. Given adequate nutrients it will grow in gravel, sand and good soils with equal success. As the late Valerie Swane would say, 'Plant it and stand back'.

Viburnum plicatum 'Mariesii'

A tall spreading deciduous shrub, often growing over 9ft (3m) tall, with distinctly tiered horizontal branches, it is covered in small light green leaves in spring and small flat, white flowers. This viburnum makes an excellent specimen plant and a sensational hedge.

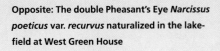

Opposite: The double Pheasant's Eye *Narcissus poeticus* var. *recurvus* naturalized in the lake-field at West Green House

Right: Tall Australian eucalyptus encircle the country gardens at Kennerton Green

4 | yellows, pinks and browns

Color is a very useful tool to tie different parts of a garden together. Designers often use large groupings of one plant placed at regular intervals to carry the eye along a border. Bulb growers often favor the trick of a river of blue *Muscari* to suggest a blue river between separate groups of brightly colored bulbs, unifying the patches of color. I have used color to tie the original and new gardens together at Kennerton Green, particularly where I needed to connect two different styles of gardening together.

The old garden is a typical Australian country garden with tall trees and gently curving lawns edged by flower beds, whereas my own ideas tend more to structural designs enclosed in garden rooms, divided by hedges, fences or groves of trees. My connecting device is principally large blocks of single color, and every so often two neighboring colors are used as contrasts. As the house, tucked into its abundant white garden, is the garden's center and all driveways and paths radiate from here, the central connecting color is white, leading first to yellow.

The first color bed starts at a fence covered by a yellow hedge of *Forsythia suspensa*, a blaze of yellow in early spring. Here I inherited clumps of King Alfred daffodils, simple primroses with *Alyssum saxatile* 'Compactum', and *A.* 'Gold Dust' a thick whipped butter border following the lawn line as the border widens. The whorls of yellow flowers above the furry green leaves of groups of

Phlomis russeliana are an excellent combination with the stiff sword leaves of *Sisyrinchium striatum*, its upright stems studded with small lemon-cream flowers. White flowers return in a group of twenty deliciously perfumed bushes including *Philadelphus* 'Beauclerk' and *P.* x *lemoinei* and *Choisya ternata*. Self-sown honesty and the yellow tulip *Tulipa* 'Golden Apeldoorn' struggle for room between them, mingling yellows among the predominantly white grouping before the new bed and next color block begins.

Right: *Tulipa* **'Maureen' flowers as the long border turns to yellow**

Below: The white borders in the old garden at Kennerton Green merge here to become a border of yellow

Opposite: Golden alyssum, *Tulipa* **'Maureen' and scillas in the blue and yellow border**

Previous page: *Viola* **'Anitque' capture the spectrum of connecting colors – yellow, pink and brown**

'My connecting device is principally large blocks of single color, and every so often two neighboring colors are used as contrasts.'

One way of breaking the eye from one color to another in a garden is to insert a block of flowering shrubs such as philadelphus to provide a firm, weighty presence to change the tempo. In a dull area choose a glossy evergreen shrub such as *Choisya ternata*; its glossy green leaves and bright white flowers will provide a dramatic punctuation mark. In a small garden this blocking effect is particularly useful. If you haven't room to use groups of plants, choose one striking example, or clip evergreens into solid statements.

The bed drifts into shades of blue, but the color here is secondary to the structure as large groups of clipped box cones, squares, balls and lollipops appear again as strong evergreen punctuation marks both in density and shapes, a foil to the soft habits of the preceding group of philadelphus. Here is not only a gentle connecting theme but formal sentinels either side of a path on its way to the geometric-shaped potager, where form is the principal statement and link, color is secondary.

My beds in blocks of white, yellow and blue stretch halfway around the garden in a rhythmic curve using many contrasting themes, topiaries and tunnels, banks of single plants, climbers and especially trees and thousands of annuals and perennials to create unification by color but surprises by design.

In warmer parts of the world brilliant yellow is clean and bright even on the hottest days, while in cooler climates it needs subduing. Under hot skies yellow has all the freshness of a long cool drink, and it is a bright light on cold days. It must

be the right color for us for our bushland is host to thousands of varieties of native wattle, every shade from cream to the rich golden-yellow of the Cootamundra wattle, *A. baileyana*. I also like clear bright yellow and sky blue together, and use them in blocks, one leading to the other.

If you baulk at a vast expanse of yellow but have a small curve in a herbaceous bed, an effective tiered planting could comprise the rich dark yellow compact *Potentilla recta* 'Warrenii' in the front, the deep brownish-maroon *Hemerocallis* 'Root Beer' behind, with a little more height added by the much more lax lemon-yellow *Coreopsis verticillata* 'Moonbeam' to provide a softening effect. If you still have space at the back try one of the dark blue monkshoods such as *Aconitum* 'Bressingham Spire', and perhaps weave the deep reddish-brown annual *Cosmos atrosanguineus* through the group.

A pleasing grouping of yellow and blue is formed by matting a bed of the useful intensely blue yellow-eyed daisy *Felicia amelloides* below a standard yellow English rose, *Rosa* 'Graham Thomas'; the colors of both plants are of equal intensity but the simple daisy shape loosens the formality of standard roses. Reaching to the sun *Verbascum olympicum* looks to be covered by soft white fur from the tip of its 6ft (2m) spire to its dramatic grey leaves. It is an inpirational plant dotted with flat yellow flowers especially if a group is allowed to seed beside a path to break a view or to hide a surprise around a corner.

A striking blue bed forms a backdrop to my long yellow tunnel which is gradually becoming covered with the climbing *Rosa* 'Golden Showers' among the golden wisteria style tresses of *Laburnum anagyroides*. Laburnum is snail heaven in my garden: hours are spent on tiptoes and ladders dislodging them from the highest cross bars, we cover the ground with snail repellent, but all to no avail, they climb to the highest branches and decimate the plant until hardly a leaf is left by the end of summer. Thankfully this passes nearly unnoticed for *R.* 'Golden Showers' is exactly the color of laburnum and blooms profusely. Some people doubted whether I should grow a mixed archway, but it has proved a practical solution as well as a pleasing combination.

If you have the space and the patience, laburnum tunnels are one of the great joys of late spring, but laburnum is a fleeting beauty, so to prolong the flowering period of such a major garden feature it is best interspersed with another climber such as the rose *R.* 'Golden Showers', each plant placed 3ft (1m) apart inside and either side of the arch so the matching plants join together. It will take at least eight years to achieve a covered laburnum tunnel, longer if the archway is across a driveway, but when complete it will be a brilliant display for a good month, a visual showstopper of golden light whatever the weather.

Rosa 'Golden Showers' blooms before the laburnum commences to flower in the archway at Kennerton Green

Beneath the arch the yellow faces of *Limnanthes douglasii* happily creep on to the gravel, in company of the bright blue *Lithospermum diffusum*. The tall clear sky blue bearded iris *I.* 'Portrait of Larrie' leans towards the center of the path with a matching dwarf iris at its feet and behind the yellow tunnel the blue beds continue. These blocks of yellow and blue continue for 18ft (6m) before meeting an embankment of white to adjust the eye to the next story.

One of the visual delights that we all know and love is the image of nasturtiums creeping across the path at Monet's garden at Giverny in France. This is tremendously easy to copy but can be very rampant. Yellow *Limnanthes douglasii* and blue *Lithospermum diffusum* look very cool and clean against a white gravel path making an informal edge. *Lysimachia nummularia* 'Aurea', Creeping Jenny, and *Thymus* x *citriodorus* 'Aureus', a golden herb are brilliant shades of yellow and gold, delight in creeping across gravel and make bright edges for summer gardens.

yellow favorites

Acacia baileyana 'Cootamundra Wattle'

Although there are hundreds of 'wattle' species, this small tree with grey ferny leaves with a hint of purple is the Australian wattle for me. Covered in brilliant gold balls of flowers each spring, it will grow in well-drained soil in Southern Australia. In England, Europe and North America it will survive in the mildest of climates.

Cephalaria gigantea

This is a perennial giant scabious with slender green stems up to 6ft (2m) tall, waving pale lemon, pincushion-shaped flowers. It likes good soil and full sun.

Fritillaria imperialis 'Lutea Maxima'

These crown imperial fritillaries are bulbs that flower in mid-spring. Tall strong green stems often up to 4ft (1.5m) tall are topped by yellow bells with a topknot of green leaves. Crown imperials will not tolerate soggy soils.

Helianthus annuus

Sunflowers are perhaps the symbol of late summer with their giant yellow flowers on 6ft (2m) high stalks. Not quite as tall as the traditional sunflower, 'Russian Giant', 'Ruby Sunset' is rust-red and new varieties come in creams and shades of yellow, gold and tawny brown.

Laburnum x watereri 'Vossii'

A slender tree with long racemes of wisteria-type yellow flowers up to 20in (50cm) long which bloom in late spring. It is superb grown in single lines over tunnels and arches. It likes well-drained, good soil, but will not tolerate soggy feet.

Phlomis fruticosa

Jerusalem sage is a hairy blue-green leaved herbaceous shrub bearing whorls of yellow flowers at regular intervals throughout summer. It is fully hardy in cool temperate areas, but may need to be cut back in autumn to ensure survival in colder temperatures.

Rosa 'Graham Thomas'

One of David Austin's most admired roses of clear rich yellow over shiny green leaves. The flowers are cup-shaped, filled with petals, and the bush is vigorous, growing up to 4ft (1.3m). To my mind this is the very best yellow rose in summer.

Rosa 'Nevada'

A modern shrub rose that grows vigorously to around 6ft (2m) by 6ft (2m). It is covered by semi-double large creamy-white flowers with prominent stamens. It is one of the earliest roses to flower and looks very good in massed plantings along a driveway.

Sisyrinchium striatum

A perennial with iris-type leaves. The small flowers are palest creamy-yellow and cluster down stems that grow to 3ft (1m) tall. It spreads well and is happiest in full sun although it will tolerate semi-shade, but not wet feet.

Sternbergia lutea

These look very similar to a spring crocus but flower in autumn. They are like brilliant yellow light bulbs under trees turning their technicolor best before the leaf carpet becomes too dense. Happy as rockery plants, they will naturalize, flowering happily in full sun or some light shade.

Opposite: Rosa 'Golden Showers' has proved a good rose happily confronting climatic excesses. The flower is raggedy in appearance fading gently from gold as it ages

'. . . I couldn't plant an English garden without the acknowledged presence of at least a hint of pink . . .'

Pinks at West Green

Soft English light is perfectly complemented by pink, which warms the light respectfully, providing a gentle visual glow even when the sun fails to appear. However my hand at first trembled at pink, and my plant lists at West Green House planned for rich purples, burgundy, blues and mauves. I didn't think entire beds of pink flowers could be planted so close to bricks where tones of orange and ochre dominated. But I felt I couldn't plant an English garden without the acknowledged presence of at least a hint of pink, it had to include pink roses and groups of lupins, foxgloves, peonies, lilies and pink tinged magnolias.

I looked very closely at the walls and detected a purple pigment in some of the Hampshire brick firings, so I took heart and tentatively tried to introduce a little pink to make the transition from mauve to white. The last plants of the mauve border already hint at pink: the pink-mauve *Delphinium* 'Astolat', the silver lilac balls of *Allium cristophii*, and a daylily of pinkish-mauve *Hemerocallis* 'Catherine Woodbery'. These lead into a developing cool pink bed which weaves towards flowers of white; it starts with the flourish of the striped red and white Bourbon rose *Rosa* 'Variegata di Bologna', and the pale pink and crimson striped hybrid perpetual *R.* 'Ferdinand Pichard'. I have planted groups of pink roses: my favorite soft pink *R.* 'Königin von Dänemark', the delicate pink *R.* 'Fantin-Latour', the quaint blooms of the sumptuous pink Centifolia rose *R.* 'Ispahan', and Bourbon roses *R.* 'Louise Odier' , *R.* 'Madame Isaac Pereire' and *R.* 'Reine Victoria', cups of pink petals. These are the underplanting for standard balls of *Lonicera*, honeysuckle species of cream and deep pink.

Many spreading and wayward plants are now available such as sophisticated pom pom trees, all shaped and clipped to form standard flowering balls in spring. Trees of *Lonicera*, *Weigela*, lilacs or lavenders can all add contrast in texture, color, form and structure above waves of soft perennials. In smaller beds standards can look most effective when grown in generous containers.

All these large shapes needed a film to break down the feeling of sugar icing, so drifts of *Linaria purpurea* 'Canon Went' curtained the entire bed. This looked wonderful the first year, but soon had the denseness of a picket fence of very pale pink flowers to be severely weeded each spring. Solid pink and white lupins, *Lupinus* 'The Chatelaine', were parted by waves of *Aquilegia* 'Heidi ', pretty pink granny's bonnets, and the sturdy spires of *Verbascum chaixii* 'Pink Domino' pushed their way through the thick groups of roses. As I became more courageous, the bed became pinker, *Digitalis* x *mertonensis* arrived as did *Sidalcea* 'Rose Queen'. I loved the spikes of the wafer thin round flowers clinging to their waving spikes, but it was far too definite a pink to be tolerated by any red brick wall, so only a few strands remain, the bulk replaced with *Phlox maculata* 'Omega', white with a softish pink eye.

The beds at West Green must respect the old knee high hedges to the path so planting tends to be tall, but on the lawn side I have placed *Paeonia* 'Shirley Temple', the flowers just scoops of pink and white ice cream beside *P.* 'Lady Alexandra McDuff', deep pink frills filled with loose white petals. Clumps of the delicate hearts of pink *Dicentra spectabilis* nod above soft green foliage interspersed by the white variety. *Diascia fetcaniensis* is another prolifically flowered small pink flower, and I have planted it next to groups of *Hosta plantaginea* var. *japonica* with its sweetly smelling white flowers. The green *Zinnia elegans* 'Envy' adds zest in high summer.

The garden was reassuring, a cottage garden ambience, but it still worried me. The style of the house, the parterres, the follies, all have dramatic pretensions far removed from the spirit of unsophisticated pink. So in went leaves of burgundy, port and Shiraz to strengthen the confection.

The wine colored leaves and stems of red mountain spinach *Atriplex hortensis* and the tall thick stems and flat burgundy red leaves of *Angelica gigas* create deep colored backdrops to the pathside planting. Low mounds of *Heuchera* 'Palace Purple' and 'Pewter Moon', both with portwine leaves, glow richly bringing a depth and stability to the planting. *Monarda* 'Beauty of Cobham' boasts flowers in a mixture of burgundy and sugar pink, echoed in the honeysuckle which clambers over a tripod, and these tones introduce a necessary sophistication to the pinks.

Opposite: *Verbascum* 'Jackie' and *Ranunculus* 'Nearly Black' backed by flowers of black and pink at Kennerton Green

Left: Hot pink spikes of *Sidalcea* 'Rose Queen' at West Green House

pink favorites

Digitalis x mertonensis

A large, crushed strawberry foxglove growing up to 4ft (1.2m) tall. It likes a rich moist soil and will flower happily in semi-shade from late spring to early autumn.

Linaria purpurea 'Canon Went'

This toadflax is a self-seeding perennial of tall, delicate spikes, covered in small pale pink flowers to resemble a tiny snapdragon. It grows to around 3ft (1m), flowering all summer in full sun, but tolerating semi-shade and poor soils.

Malus floribunda

One of the earliest blossom trees to flower each spring, when its tight bright pink buds open to shell pink flowers, with a mass of petals attracting hundreds of bees. Trees grow to around 33ft (10m) in cool districts, with autumn color but insignificant fruit.

Paeonia 'Sarah Bernhardt'

This is an old favorite, a large double peony, that is nearly a globe of ruffled petals of pure pink. Luscious blooms appear in midsummer on stems to around 3ft (1m) tall. Peonies like full sun in good soil.

Papaver orientale 'Turkish Delight'

The largest poppy I've grown, it's candy pink flowers are supported on strong, furry stems up to 3ft (1m). Plant it towards the back of the border as it leaves a large gap when cut back in midsummer.

Tulipa 'Webber's Parrot'

One of the prettiest pastel tulips, this ivory white Parrot tulip has very frilly edges that are a mauve-tinged pink with slashes of green. Flowering in late spring, plants may grow as tall as 20in (50cm). These tulips are overwintered at West Green House, but lifted and discarded in less temperate climates.

Wisteria floribunda 'Kuchi-beni'

Long racemes of white flowers with just a suggestion of pink may be 18in (45cm) long. In warmer areas this is a strong growing plant but in England it often takes several years to flower. Grow this wisteria in full sun.

Left: Daring pink cosmos colonize a corner in the pink border at West Green House

Opposite: *Lonicera giganten* 'Superba' and *Rosa* 'Königin von Dänemark' capture an old garden's spirit in a border of sugar pink plants

Brown

The warm tones of brown are ideal for linking all kinds of pinks and copper colors through to mellow yellows. When I first saw *Rosa* 'Julia's Rose', my love affair with brown plants began. It is a modern hybrid tea, the color of a cappuccino, with copper-brown buds opening to a large warm parchment flower. In some lights it looks flushed with slate, in others faded copper-pink; it seemed to demand I create a bed to complement it.

I began my brown collection with the New Zealand flax *Phormium* 'Maori Sunrise', tall flat swords of brown-bronze leaves touched with pink and red, and bronze fennel, which has brown feathers exactly the color I wanted, although it is a wilful self-seeder. Three of the most beautiful brown-toned plants are verbascums. The tall coppery *Verbascum* 'Helen Johnson', the slightly paler *V.* 'Cotswold Queen' and the small growing more branched *V.* 'Jackie', pale caramel with a darker eye. Another favorite is the rusty foxglove *Digitalis ferruginea*, its tall spikes surrounded by lesser stems covered in thousands of tiny brown bells look splendid rising behind lush low-growing leaves of *Heuchera* 'Chocolate Ruffles'.

Brown flowers are among spring's earliest. Dusty brown-tinged hellebores emerge just as winter seems to be going on for ever. *Fritillaria persica* is a mixture of wine and dark greenish-brown it's a mysterious plant, I've only been able to grow it in cooler climates, although fritillaries will grow in the coolest areas of Australia and South Africa. Iris come in all shades of rust and browns. *Iris* 'Chocolate Vanilla' is warm brown and slate white, flowering in late spring upstaging

everything else in the bed. The bearded iris *I.* 'Langport Duchess' is the color of milky coffee flecked with grated nutmeg; I've planted this at West Green House but its subdued murky tones are not everyone's taste. Another favorite is the species iris *I.* 'Holden Clough', its yellow petals curving out with deep purple veins, resembling the long brownish legs of a hairy spider.

Murky browns make great conversation points in a garden bed. Just for the fun of it try a succession of them through the seasons. Begin with *Fritillaria persica* in early spring, followed by stinking hellebores *Helleborus foetidus*, black lilies – perhaps a cobra-like purple and brown striped *Arisaema triphyllum* and the dark browns and creams of *Iris tuberosa*. The naked twisting stems of *Corylus avellana* 'Contorta' provides extra mysterious presence through winter.

Brown with pinks

I thought of trying a brown garden bed in both Kennerton Green and West Green House. Groups of *R.* 'Julia's Rose', the perennials and the bronze leaved plants went into both gardens. In Australia the bed bordered the driveway, so to soften the edges 'Antique' pansies with faces of gold, black, parchment, brown and old rose were tucked beneath clipped cubes of berberis – I purchased a variety known as *Berberis* 'Firecracker', similar to *B. thunbergii* 'Rose Glow', its new shoots a brilliant mottled pink above the older dull bronze leaves.

In spring the copper and bronze tones looked shiny and very unusual grouped together, but by midsummer in Mittagong I hated the faded brown leaves above dry brown beds all edged by burnt brittle lawn. The roses were faded by the light into colorlessness, it was all utterly depressing. However I noted that where there were black or old-rose colored violas still flowering, they reflected their color into adjoining brown leaves, giving life to a group. So the bed was given a twelve month reprieve and the following autumn plants of black, lush raspberry and a splash of white joined the currently unpopular browns.

Left: The brown rose *R.* 'Julia's Rose'

Above: The thousands of tiny brown bells that cover *Digitalis ferruginea* by summer

The following spring *Digitalis* x *mertonensis* shot spikes through my Australian bed – its crushed strawberry bells pushing through the stiff flax, emphasising the brownish-pink on the leaves, with drifts of pink forget-me-not beneath. *Dianthus barbatus* 'Nigrescens' jostled to be seen, heads of tiny velvet flowers the color of the dregs in a Shiraz bottle, along with the dark red pincushions of *Scabiosa atropurpurea* 'Ace of Spades', all planted in very bold clumps of seven or eleven plants. A luscious raspberry and white antirrhinum was suggested and I experimented with a new *Gaura lindheimeri*, its dark stems disguised beneath bright pink butterfly flowers.

The brilliant summer skies of hotter climates drain and dull the bronze-browns, but when they are supported by plants of rich pink to complement brown toned leaves, as well as a few good groups of blackish plants, the dark depths create a rich paisley, a brown-pink brocade. The overall effect is a border of quiet glamour. I love it all and it has become my favorite bed.

Brown grasses

There is one group of brown plants I cannot grow, grasses. They may currently be the epitome of garden chic, treasured in the cooler areas of Europe and extremely suitable climatically for most gardens in warmer areas, but I do not like to grow them – although I do make an occasional exception. Every Australian country child is warned not to walk through long brown grass in summer, not to poke around clumps of bamboo or pampas grass as they are the habitat of snakes, nasty brown or black ones with their friends and relations, copperheaded varieties and blacks with red bellies. Of course it's all in the mind, but I still associate grasses with reptiles. Additionally, long brown grass and thistles near the house are taboo in country or bushland Australia as combustible dry grass explodes when touched by fire during the dry season. Quite apart from this, I admit I do find long clumps of spiky grass foreign, intruding upon and unrelated to a classical herbaceous border where grasses seem out of style and rhythm. When I see them I have to resist a compulsive urge to pull them out. Like a bowl of daffodils proudly displayed in Singapore, I find grasses in a border out of place and unnecessary.

Left: A lively border of unusual color combinations of brown, pinks and blacks at Kennerton Green

Brown with peach

Brown needs other colors around it to exploit its depth and in England my brown bed looked respectable but not inspiring in its first year. For two seasons I played with color combinations. White with brown reminded me of the two-tone golf shoes, so the white was removed. Clumps of black plants were dull, then I tried the blush pink English rose *R*. 'Heritage', which was pretty but far too insipid. I needed a glowing color like the cool warmth of glow worms or the pale flame in a fire, soft warm peach or a not too yellow apricot. Peach is too ethereal under hot skies, but in mellow light it is beautiful with browns.

To the tall brown foxgloves and verbascums I have added *Achillea* 'Salmon Beauty'. Its flat heads rise above feathery foliage which adds much needed bulk to a bed planted with predominantly spiky plants. These include the skyscrapers of the plant world *Eremurus robustus* with their tiny rows of pale peach flowers, and the darker *Eremurus* x *isabellinus* 'Cleopatra'. The lupin 'Peach' and the bearded peachy-pink iris *I*. 'Edward of Windsor' supply good color, but the most important addition to the original plants are the new brown roses.

Bill le Grice Roses in Norfolk offer roses in every shade of brown from gingerbread to hot chocolate, some flushed gold, others shot with rose and slate, many worth trying to find out which colors are happiest here. *Rosa* 'Julia's Rose' is not a strong growing bush, so now I tend to crowd her, gratefully accepting the spray of blooms that appear among the perennials. This rose is a beautiful bonus rather than a main event, a rose that needs companions to reflect and enhance her color, their choice depending on the light and latitude.

Achillea is an excellent plant, easy to grow with delightful grey-green ferny foliage which clumps beautifully and hides lots of brown earth, and flat heads of flowers rising up at different levels between spiky plants. Try mixing terracotta and orangey-brown varieties in the front of a yellow border to tone it down.

I have come quite recently to brown plants, yet some of my garden's most evocative images are brown – browns backlit by the long low beams of autumn sun, stands of seed heads, black-brown sedums, silver-brown balls of alliums, the rusty lace ruffs of *Hydrangea paniculata*. At Kennerton the ferny foliaged *Metasequoia glyptostroboides* stands like a magnificent rusty pyramid in autumn, having changed color through the seasons from brilliant pale lime to mid-green climaxing in rust-red. Hedges of paper brown hornbeams were a cultural shock when I first came to England, they looked so untidy, but now I rejoice in their warm color as I learn to observe and love a winter's landscape and not to buy an airline ticket as soon as the autumn leaves mess begins.

Right: Tall spires of *Verbascum* 'Helen Johnson', *Eremurus robustus* and *Digitalis ferruginea* surround the old well head at West Green House

brown favorites

Cosmos atrosanguineus

Often called the chocolate cosmos, this is said to be a perennial, but I find I treat it as an annual in cooler climates. The flower grows to 18in (40cm) tall and is a black-brown with a reddish glow and smells of chocolate. It requires a rich soil and sun and flowers from late summer into autumn.

Digitalis ferruginea

A perennial light brown foxglove that can grow to 6ft (2m) tall, covered by hundreds of light brown tiny bells. It grows happily in sun, semi-shade and shade, flowering from late spring in warm climates but midsummer in cooler areas.

Fritillaria persica

I often feel this is the most mysterious plant in the garden in spring – beautiful black-brown bells hang in pyramid shapes on slim stems up to 4ft (1.2m) high. These secretive, understated flowers have a drop dead elegance. Grow them in rich soil in a sunny spot.

Iris 'Chocolate Vanilla'

This iris often reaches 4ft (1.2m) tall, with all the delicious appeal of a two toned chocolate bar. The tops are slate white, encircled by lower petals of rich chocolate brown. Flowering in mid-spring it likes full sun and will tolerate heat.

Rosa 'Buff Beauty'

A beautiful hybrid Musk rose of yellow, its deeper buds fading to flowers of buff. I like this rose planted in groups and underplanted by Verbascum 'Jackie' – a good matching of color. The flowers are a medium-sized semi-double and bloom profusely.

Rosa 'Edith Holden'

I am captivated by the range of brown roses now available and this is a Floribunda rose of russet-brown. It appears to be a strong growing bush worthy of a front-of-the-border position. Like all roses it needs well mulched soil to achieve abundant summer flowering.

Verbascum 'Helen Johnson'

Think of a verticle line of burnished small copper pans, this is the color and effect of this amazingly colored verbascum. The 4ft (1.2m) tall stems have a grey-green felted look, a soft foil for the flowers studded down the stem. Verbascums flower throughout summer into autumn and tolerate poorish soil.

Opposite: *Iris* **'Chocolate Vanilla' beside the croquet lawn at Kennerton Green**

5 | green

'. . . It was the cool oasis of trees rather than the flowers that provided the memory of a pleasant afternoon.'

Green gardens masquerade under many forms. I remember as a child my mother and grandmother returning from a midsummer visit to a country garden, languidly discussing the fine deciduous trees surrounding the homestead. It was the cool oasis of trees rather than the flowers that provided the memory of a pleasant afternoon.

The trees planted half a century ago dominate the country garden at Kennerton Green. These are a fine if haphazard collection, many planted to mark a specific occasion such as the excitement of Princess Margaret's visit, a Colonial Governor coming to lunch, a birthday. They include many contrasting shades and shapes of green such as the huge lime leaves of *Paulownia tomentosa*, the foxglove tree, an acid contrast to neighboring darker English elms; the striking green and white *Acer negundo* 'Variegatum', and the tulip tree *Liriodendron tulipifera* with its dark green saddle-shaped leaves and green tulips edged in orange as though quickly dipped in paint. *Metasequoia glyptostroboides* is one of the garden's giants, its feathery leaves the palest green in spring and rust in autumn, while the aptly named maidenhair tree *Ginkgo biloba* is the most ancient species.

Spring is officially announced for me when the crimson buds of the *Malus floribunda* explode among young green leaves into a cloud of pearl pink blossoms overhung by thousands of humming bees, and the season departs with the last petals of *Malus Ioensis,* its sprays of cupped pink blooms succumbing to the first hot days of summer. Nyssas change from green to become the stars of autumn, with leaves like colored ribbons, while liquidambars turn to bursts of burgundy, fire and yellow.

When I think of other green gardens I picture the giant trees so beloved by Victorian gardeners planted as exotic backdrops in English gardens. Or I see the grey-greens of an Australian native bush garden, an olive green Mediterranean landscape, the lush tropical green captured in pots in a Thai courtyard, or the leathery elephant ears of hostas in every shade of green from grey to lime as showstoppers in a European border.

There are so many green gardens, all so different in concept and geography. For many, green gardens are symbolized by the glories of 17th century France, where the great patterns of grass, hedge and forest are viewed with awe by the tourist trudging the grounds of Vaux le Vicomte or Versailles against piercing winds, or trying to find shelter from too hot sun.

I was enchanted when I saw the small West Green House parterre. It had the design elements of the grand baroque gardens and at times of contemplation I imagine gentlemen with wigs and red heels adding color to the green. But green gardens with topiary reach back into classical antiquity, praised by Pliny the Younger in the first century BC. He describes his villa, 'in front of the colonnade is a terrace laid out with box hedges clipped into different shapes from which a bank slopes down, also with figurines of animals…'

Above: The parterre gardens capture the spirit of another age at West Green House

Opposite: The cool allure of twin avenues of pleached Hornbeam trees rising above hedges of box at West Green House

Previous page: *Tulipa* **'Spring Green'**

Green structure

The little West Green parterre is the most romantic design of heart shapes punctuated with topiaries of lollipops, cones and standards all set in low knarled hedges of box. The area covered is a square of 62ft (19m) by 40ft (12m), enclosed by ivy-clad brick walls painted with white flowers in spring and summer. Today's design was the work of Robert Weir Schulz, around 1898. It was originally filled with roses but they are long gone and it is now simplified to small green hedges and white gravel. It is a garden that relies on its geometry of ordered calm to create a restful green picture, timeless, romantic and tranquil. Six dark green hollies like upright arrows lead the eye beyond the inner wall to a second walled parterre also of simplisitic design, twenty two sunken lead tanks outlined in neat box hedged squares of 3ft (1m) x 2ft (60cm) brimming with pads of deep green water lilies which shy white flowers peep from in the English summer.

If you plant a parterre in an enclosed area surrounded by high walls or hedges you may choose to graduate the heights of your plants to create interest and balance. In my lilypond parterre I have placed sentinels of clipped yew and lollipops of densely clipped hollies, shapes of varying height to lead the eye from the high brick walls gradually down to the small hedged ponds in the smartly raked gravel. The contrasts between the textures and different shades of green are marked by the broad shining lily pads nestling amidst the neat, miniature box.

Opposite: Pristine white lilies flower from rows of tanks in the water lily parterre

Top: Parterres were popular in early American gardens. Here, one of similar style breaks the glare of white gravel

Top left: Lollipop-shaped holly trees reflect light from their shiny leaves

Below left: Midsummer *Lilium* bring polished light to the walled garden in Hampshire

Above: The gold tasselled pavilion in the water lily parterre awaits the arrival of its resident chickens

Lightening formal shapes

Walled enclosures can feel rather hard and I am trying to break the nearly too sharp feeling of the high brick walls, hard gravel and clipped lines to provide a much lighter edge in such a confined space. So I have draped the walls with all white roses, *Rosa* 'Long John Silver' a hybrid climber, and the vigorous ramblers *R.* 'Seagull' and *R.* 'Sanders' White Rambler'. Narrow border beds below the walls are now filled with all white flowers, green and white tulips in spring, followed by white herbaceous peonies and lilies for glamour.

My lilies begin with the pure white Asiatic lily *Lilium* 'Mont Blanc' in early summer, followed by white Regal lilies. *L. regale* flower until the height of summer and Oriental hybrids such as the pure white *L.* 'Casa Blanca' continue the theme throughout. From late in the season until autumn Tiger lilies such as the creamy-white *L.* 'Sweet Surrender' complete the story for summer-long flowering of these exotic flowers.

Any bare space in the beds has had *Nicotiana* 'Lime Green' tucked in, its single star shaped flowers luminous and very effective below the drama of the lilies.

My love of geometry needs still more subtle tweaking as I tend towards the severe shapes. Another softening element in this parterre are the chickens in a stylish pavilion, a romantic gesture at the end of the garden, its roof of stripes and gold tin tassels a focal point enlivened by much clucking, fluffing and strutting. Although this chicken house is fun and the parterre dramatically plain, together it is a stylish fantasy using plants and shapes always associated with classical gardens, its personality harmonizing with the traditional elements throughout the gardens.

I am always most impressed on a summer's day by the sight of the glossy green shining from box, holly or tall lily leaves. They seem the perfect accessories to wax white blooms. For a small smart modern parterre try the great French couturier Chanel's signature flower, the autumn flowering white *Camellia sasanqua* with thick dark shiny leaves that can be clipped to make excellent hedges, while the miniature varieties like *C. sasanqua* 'Little Liane' make stunning small leaved hedges covered with compact white flowers in autumn and early winter. In frost-free climates this glossy green effect can be achieved with the bonus of the glorious perfumed flowers by planting gardenia hedges.

Contrasting parterres

The design of the Australian cottage is more in sympathy with a pre-Revolution American cottage. When constructing a parterre here I was unknowingly probably looking at the same patterns that American colonial gardeners used when they created their small cottage gardens. It uses the elements of an Anglo-Dutch garden, but in its simplest form: a plain rectangle of box hedging 25ft (8m) by 12ft (4m) with box balls and cones placed at regular intervals, dissected in quarters by a diagonally curving line. A topiary bird of unknown breed sits in a central urn; it may be a peacock or a fantail pigeon, shaped from 'Muehlenbeckia' a fine leaved fast growing creeper, only to be let loose if contained in a pot. Here it is covering a frame of the statuesque bird, providing what I think is a necessary quirky note. The parterre has proved an excellent way to provide a simple but smart green and white charm to the cottage entrance, and the dark green box absorbs the light and cuts the glare of the surrounding white gravel to an acceptable level.

Many gardeners veer away from box, thinking it slow to grow and hard to maintain, but neither is true. Box is an exceptional plant, at home climatically from subtropical to cool temperate gardens, a bold green statement that maintains its chic good looks independent of the seasons. I still find English box, *Buxus sempervirens*, with its small smooth pointed leaves, is the most compact plant for clipped edges or parterres. The Japanese box *B. microphylla* var. *japonica* grows more

quickly, a taller plant with a larger rounded leaf that is quite acid green in new growth but darkens with age. Leave this plant for taller hedges, otherwise after trimming, every leaf seems to have been clipped in half. In warmer climates dwarf box *B. sempervirens* 'Suffruticosa' is gaining in popularity as it requires minimal maintenance.

To introduce a parterre was a foreign design element in my traditional Australian garden, so the surrounding beds needed to be formalized and edged by box hedging to integrate the new idea. To one side I divided the borders with zigzag lines of box with sculptural balls of *Pittosporum tenuifolium,* hebe, santolina, *Teucrium fruticans* and rosemary in the parterre design. Espalier Granny Smith apples on free standing goblet frames repeated the idea of formality on a second side, but the third side became a long pattern of interlocking triangles and filled in zigzags of aromatic grey-green rosemary and lavender. This forms a permanent mat of mauve and blue, a decorative pattern for a dry sun baked spot.

Grey-green foliaged plants are often the most drought-tolerant, perfect for dry ridges and terraces, which need not be the Cinderella spots of the garden. By choosing a range of drought-tolerant Mediterranean shrubs and perennials, and using a small hedge trimmer, a most sophisticated garden can emerge. Plant a grouping of favorite green-grey plants, perhaps cistus, rosemary, lavender, teucrium, santolina or artemisia,

and clip them into rounded and conical shapes. Vary the heights between 18in (50cm) and 3ft (1m), with one or two slightly higher, and the result is garden sculpture, an elegant planting of shapes and textures creating harmonies of soft light and shade.

Opposite: By midsummer the old borders at West Green House are predominantly filled with green and white plants

Below: Box shaped as a corkscrew adds height, design and structure to the garden

Patterns in dull greens

Beyond the original garden at Kennerton Green was a small field slightly smaller than a bowling green but quite large enough for a grass tennis court, completely enclosed by a collection of different cypresses, all at least 20ft (7m) tall and dense enough to act as windbreaks in the winter months. I decided to make a modern parterre there, a green garden that used different textures and shapes to create a cool space. The excellent Australian nurserywoman Joan Arnold had a collection of about 80 bay trees *Laurus nobilis* that I had long coveted. Some had trunks trained as corkscrews, others straight, all about 4½ft (1.5m) tall. This idea became the basis of my bay tree garden.

I based my original plan on a French garden I had seen in a magazine, a courtyard of squares with each square devoted to a single plant variety. My design was a grid of eight equal oblong beds edged in box. These in turn were outlined by a grid of the 80 bay trees clipped as lollipops to a height of 5ft (1.75m) tall, their feet encircled in box rings. An established 10ft (3m) tall bay tree found behind the chicken yard was removed to become the centerpiece, its feet a circular mat of box 9ft (3m) across or 36ft (12m) round.

Unless you have plenty of help in a garden, keep a parterre simple. Some ideas, such as a clipped bay tree surrounded by a circle of box, work much better on a small scale – it's a crazy idea for 81 trees, but looks marvellous as the centerpiece of a small parterre, or a single design feature in a small garden.

Bay and box are tough plants that look immaculate all year round, ideal for busy town gardeners with limited garden maintenance time. Although a shaped plant must be trimmed from time to time, the idea of five clipped bay trees encircled in box laid out as a simple cross would be a smart solution for a town house, courtyard or basement garden. Surrounded with paving of stone, terracotta or gravel, it makes an eye-catching, low maintenance, minimalistic design. I'd enclose the perimeter with a green hedge perhaps of *Choisya ternata* to tie the design together.

The eight beds were designed to house balls of white marguerites but the wind proved too strong and lifted them like tumbleweed. Currently I plan a

seasonal progression commencing with *Tulipa* 'Maureen' which opens cream fading to white followed by white ranunculus, then white aquilegias, marguerites and *Penstemon* 'White Bedder'. The garden triumphs in midsummer when hundreds of Christmas lilies, *Lilium longiflorum*, bend their white trumpets nearly to the grass creating a medieval fantasy, their perfume overpowering. But the overall impression is the play of light on green in shapes, on leaves and on grass. It gives a precise crisp sensation by day, a moody pattern of shaped shadows by late afternoon.

The bay tree garden is made up of predominantly dull greens: the 81 round standards of bay leaves, the dull grey-green of the surrounding cypresses, so different from the shiny geometry of my parterre in England. It needs the introduc-

tion of sparkling light, and I am adding glitter to my greens with water in a long canal, a water staircase capturing the white and blue of the sky to lift the background of dull green.

You can add sparkle to dull greens in shade or sun with a ribbon or river of green leaves splashed with white, such as the ivy *Hedera helix* 'Glacier', or a covering of bright white flowers. The perennial viola, *Viola cornuta* 'Lambley White', flowers from spring to autumn, their cheerful round white faces at home in cool and less temperate climates, unfazed by midsummer sun.

Left: The many shades of atmospheric green in the bay tree garden at Kennerton Green

Opposite: *Echinacea purpurea* 'White Swan' stand tall in a late summer border

'. . . a moody pattern of shaped shadows by late afternoon.'

Above: Espaliered Granny Smith Apple
trees filter the warm Australian light

Main picture: *Euphorbia amygdaloides*,
the color of lime, provide a welcome
highlight in any bed of green on green

Opposite: Sprays of pale *Helleborus
foetidus* create textured contrast in
an all-green garden

Previous page: The first white flowers of
winter: snow drops bravely peep through
the frozen earth at West Green House

Light shades of green

A huge range of green plants could be used as infills for a garden. Don't underestimate the stylish effect of green on green. *Helleborus augustifolius* 'Corsicus' adds stiff light green, and mounds of *Alchemilla mollis* give a froth of acid green flowers over attractive soft greyer-green leaves, wonderful for cool gardens. Climate permitting, the Pineapple lily *Eucomis bicolor* could be fun, it flowers in late summer, with its thick stems supporting lime green blooms, with leaves bunched on top just like a pineapple! Green plants alone can give tonal messages of light green, grey-green or dark green and texture images of crispness or sharpness.

The play of green on green, of foliage on grass, can be more subtle than the traditional style of green parterre enclosed by gravel. In a cool climate it is very effective to infill the beds of a parterre with huge mounds of green hostas, their shapes and textures of green emphasising a cool mood. The waxy pale green leaves and perfumed white flowers of *Hosta plantaginea* var. *japonica* would be my first choice, a very serene plant.

A story book parterre

'If you open a garden in England you must have a tea room', I was told. The idea filled me with dread, for the thought of trying to make edible cakes was my idea of a nightmare. Perhaps this conversation took place as I first viewed the top walled garden at West Green House. For behind the high walls the entire space was consumed by a swimming pool in terminal decay, its bottom filled with debris, the concrete cracks crammed with weed and filth. Beside this dank hole a roofless and rotting gardeners' bothy added the final note of depression and so for two years its gate to the old orchard through which our future garden visitors would enter remained firmly shut.

I'm not sure where the inspiration for this corner of the garden came from. Perhaps it was the nagging worry of what to do with the ugly pool area, perhaps it was the dread of serving teas, but gradually, like Alice, I came to the end of the tunnel and as all the elements of Lewis Carroll's wonderful story were remembered and I knew my new garden would be an Alice garden, a wonderful place for a Mad Hatter's Tea Party. 'There was a table set out under the tree in front of the house and the March hare and the Hatter were having tea. A dormouse was sitting between them fast asleep.'

The story inspired the transformation of the old bothy into a kitchen and the pool became a courtyard garden of strong but simple elements, a limited number of select plant species, a color range related to the roses of the story. This created a sweet childlike statement that was planted for pure enjoyment of an impression of a

very English story, the exact place to sit and partake of a traditional English afternoon tea.

As all the walled gardens at West Green House are basically formal parterres that was also the plan for this garden, the old garden once again dictating new ideas. The newest parterre is a chess board, its squares outlined in box, its base gravel, its perspective slightly sunken for tea-time visitors to sit and look down on topiary characters of the White Rabbit, the Mad Hatter, a tea pot and the hookah-smoking Caterpillar on the mushroom. These are beautifully made frames gradually filling with box or fine ivy, set in the box-framed squares.

No Alice in Wonderland garden could be complete without reference to the Queen, so the checkerboard is lined on three sides by standard roses, the good red floribunda rose *Rosa* 'Remembrance' and a bright white rose *R.* 'Saint John', both suggested by rosarian Peter Harkness. Beneath the roses box is clipped into the pawns with balls, spirals, cones, animals and birds, and the earth covered with silver plants that will cope with the dry gravel. And to soften the starkness *Dianthus* 'Devon General' matches the red roses and *D.* 'Devon Dove' the white; the annual *Senecio maritima* 'Silver Dust' has long clumps of lacy silver-grey leaves in summer, *Alyssum* 'Snow Carpet' has bedded itself into all the cracks along with large clumps of strawberries, which look inviting beside bright red tea tables. The walls are welcoming red and white roses, the brilliant deep red climber *Rosa* 'Dublin Bay' and pure white *R.* 'White Cloud'. Rose bushes crowd the gate, double blood red *R.* 'Lilli Marlene' and old white

'. . . like Alice, I came to the end of the tunnel . . .'

Left and below: Newly planted box is beginning to fill the wire shapes of the Mad Hatter and the teapot in the Alice garden at West Green House

Opposite: Nearly all the flowers in the Alice garden are red – roses, lilies, clematis, peonies and dianthus

Rugosa roses transplanted here, a simpler form of flower. Above all this stands the 8ft (2.5m) Queen, the box already filling her skirt, her finger pointing at those that enter.

To truly reflect the Alice theme I had to find a way to include many of the brilliant red flowers shining out of the catalogues in my newly created garden. So I have made a container garden around the tea tables for midsummer crammed with the darkest of red blooms including *Verbena* 'Lawrence Johnston', *Nicotiana* x *sanderae* and *Pelargonium* 'Lord Bute' placed towards the edges, with the center containers filled to brimming with *Antirrhinum* majus 'Black Prince', and *Dianthus barbatus* 'Nigrescens'. These are placed alongside pots of white flowers.

When I first arrived at West Green House many cuttings were taken from the old box hedges so that we could repair the existing parterres. Within four years I had enough sturdy young plants to plant my checkerboard, so in every respect this new garden is in total harmony with our existing parterres. But the greatest bonus has been my neighbor who has relieved me of the trauma of 'The Mad Hatter's Tea Party' as she organizes everything beautifully and delights our visitors with anecdotes about Alice – as her grandmother was the original Alice!

Green flowers for shafts of light

While green is largely used to create structure in the garden, the long white border at Kennerton Green eventually runs into a curve of green flowers, a new border is 450ft (150m) long, dominated by fifty year old mature trees, casting in places the densest shade, denying water to penetrate, greedy to take their share of the annual mulch. Perhaps I am stretching the imagination a trifle far, as 'green' flowers are often an amalgamation of white, green, lime and yellow, but when they are combined the effect is of shades of green limelight. In deep dry shade green flowers can look lush and liquid, and lime green will light the darkest places.

I keep trying to grow the acid green *Alchemilla mollis*, the mainstay of every English gentlewoman's garden, but it is just too hot for it in sunnier climates, so the border's edge has thankfully been taken over by *Euphorbia polychroma*, wonderful domes of intense lime green that last till autumn. Large mounds of lime green helichrysum grow all year in our shade to form a luminous ground cover, a stunning backing for *Hemerocallis* 'Missouri Beauty', its citrus yellow flowers lit with green.

Lime green is a dazzling color in shade, its intense cool glow entices the eye. The lime-sherbert leaved shrub *Physocarpus opulifolius* 'Dart's Gold' revels in the gloomiest conditions, as does *Garrya elliptica*, perfect in any garden, its long yellowy-green catkins a particular joy above sulphur daffodils in early spring.

I like to repeat flowers and themes wherever possible around the garden, introducing special plants to different border escorts. The cream flowering *Sisyrinchium striatum* is one; clumped among bearded iris it harmonizes colors and shapes, continuing the progression of flowing swords throughout spring and summer. There is no true green bearded iris but there are variants of creamy-whites with veins of greens, like *Iris* 'Celestial Ballet', or whites with acid citrus falls, or with green splashes as in the dwarf iris *I.* 'Green Spot'.

The green white story can stretch for nine months a year, beginning with winter snowdrops, varieties of *Galanthus nivalis*, and the lime green flowers of *Helleborus foetidus* which bloom from late winter into spring. These plants make huge dark architectural mounds of heavily incised leaves. Green and white bell-shaped flowers include the nodding bells of *Allium triquetrum* and the *Tulipa* 'Spring Green', a must-have in a cold spring climate. Follow these with hummocks of *Astrantia major subsp. involucrata* 'Shaggy' with its pointed ruff of green bracts and white center, speckled green bunches of tiny flowers.

Of course I use green annuals: at the front of the border, the ice green and white *Euphorbia marginata*, a bushy plant with upper leaves of white and green stripes, the light lime stems of *Nicotiana* 'Starship' and the large flowers of *Zinnia elegans* 'Envy' for tall summer green.

The most simple of green gardens are formed from the placement of grass and trees as in the serene green theater at West Green House

Behind them are the tall spikes of the Irish green bells of *Moluccella laevis*. Stretching a point, I have put the perennial *Echinacea purpurea* 'White Swan' at the back of the border; although white, it looks more greeny-white by autumn, its center starts life as a green cone, turning brown with age. These spectacular daisy-shape flowers are echoed by the tall erect zinnias.

These colors are reflected again in the greeny-cream flowers of *Pieris japonica* 'Temple Bells' its bronze-green leaves polished like oriental lacquer, catching and reflecting the light in dark corners. In the deepest and coolest recess of my green border sits a colony of lush green cobra-headed arum lilies *Zantedeschia aethiopica* 'Green Goddess', stylized flowers beloved by flower arrangers. As their striking green flowers unfurl revealing generous splashes of white, their shine is another reflection of available light.

High above, the tall tree canopy forms a desired dense shade by midsummer where day after day flocks of the screeching sulphur crested cockatoos, the brilliant red and green King parrots or the multi colored Rosellas amuse themselves with denuding a chosen branch of every leaf and twig but, when the huge jet black cockatoos hit the garden, I run for cover as cones and minor branches become missiles hurled from above.

The awning of cool shade is cast by an eclectic collection of trees which include Norfolk Island pines, *Araucaria heterophylla* and *Platanus* x *hispanica*, all reaching well over 30ft (90m) high. The spreading branches of *Magnolia denudata*, and groups of *Abies veitchii* and *Cedrus libani* subsp. *atlantica* are planted closely together, creating a dense patchwork of green overhead. The golden elm, *Ulmus glabra* 'Lutescens', is another colorful delight but avoid planting it near a house for its lime green 'flower' invades every doorway and drain.

Two spectacular plants tolerate this awning of dry shade: *Romneya coulteri*, the Californian tree poppy, with its extraordinary white basins of papery petals around the golden center, relishes gravelly dry soil. Flushed with success I've planted a congregation of five or six plants here, this mass of flowers the crescendo of summer. The grey leaved *Echium pininana* with an enormous tongue of blue flowers, often 3ft (1m) long, curves outwards towards the light in spring, its shape the most structural of garden statements unforgettable when planted in groups.

Winter light reflects from the polished leaf and flower of *Gordonia axillaris* (a shrub in cooler areas), its round blooms summoning images of perfectly 'poached eggs'. Away from inland frosts, in coastal city gardens, it's a small, evergreen, perfectly proportioned tree, ideal for small gardens. Camellias, too, like the dry shade: the large wax leaved and flowered 'White Nun', is espaliered to a dividing fence beneath two *Gingko biloba* and a *Liriodendron tulipifera*. Treated this way its evergreen foliage will give privacy and the flowers will turn towards the early spring light and all the blooms will look at you.

Gardens in the last months of summer in the southern hemisphere are predominantly green, the leaves often drab, dusty and tired just hanging there waiting for the first cool days to turn them into a carnival of red and golden autumn color. So many herbaceous plants are spent, cut back and the shrubs have become monotonous green mounds in long borders. It is now I believe that clipped topiary shapes whether geometric or quirky sustain a joyous note in a garden.

Shapes made of box, holly and *Vibernum* x *burkwoodii* are polished features especially when holding raindrops after a summer storm, while *Lonicera nitida*, 'poor man's box', bay and ivy's duller leaves can act as a foil against bushes of shiny or variegated leaves.

The late season can create a middle distance gap between an earlier floral floor and the roof of leaves, so a variety of clipped plants at different heights in clusters along a border becomes a surprise when there is nothing else to exclaim over, creating furniture for the middle distance.

For me these collection of shapes hold my long border together as connecting elements as it goes from one planting and color block to another. In winter they are the garden's chief joy, green sentinels in a bare world.

'striking green flowers unfurl revealing generous splashes of white, their shine is another reflection of available light'

Opposite: The nodding head of *Fritillaria acmopetala* brings understated elegance to the garden at Kennerton Green

Right: *Arum maculatum,* Lords and Ladies, – a bold statement of majesty

green favorites

Actinidia kolomitka

A wonderful oddity, this green twining climber has the occasional leaves painted in pink and white which turn to green as they age. It grows vigorously up to 12ft (4m) and needs a sunny space.

Eucalyptus

Known for the wonderful aroma emanating from their leaves, eucalyptus are also a visual delight. There are hundreds of varieties but thay all have grey-green foliage. They cover the length and breadth of Australia resulting in a landscape encased in perpetual hazy green.

Heuchera cylindrica 'Greenfinch'

Mounds of bright green leaves with stems of pale green flowers begin to appear in early summer, reaching 18-24in (45-60cm). In warmer areas this evergreen perennial likes dappled shade but is a sun-lover in cooler climates.

Physocarpus opulifolius 'Dart's Gold'

A lime-green leaved shrub that will grow easily in shade in the southern hemisphere. With creamy-white clusters of spring flowers it is said to grow to around 12ft (4m) but mine have not attained this height.

Nicotiana x sanderae 'Lime Green'

A midsummer annual with lime-green star-shaped flowers that gives a garden a cool luminous glow. Growing to 2ft (75cm) tall, they do need to be kept watered.

Ruta graveolens 'Jackman's Blue'

This herb forms a mound of deeply divided blue-green leaves in summer. It has insignificant yellow flowers and grows to over 12ft (4m) in full sun.

Santolina rosmarinifolia 'Primrose Gem'

The green santolina, a Mediterranean herb, will thrive in dry spots. Its bright green, delicate leaves look best when clipped – an excellent shrub which requires full sun.

Tulipa 'Spring Green'

This is a viridiflora tulip and absolutely my favorite bulb. It grows on a strong stem, 15in (45cm), and has pride of place in my spring borders. Its pure white petals are slashed with green and flare slightly at the edges.

Silybum marianum

This is a very prickly green thistle with leaves that look to have captured spider webs in a white and green design. It is very effective at a garden's edge producing a good mound of around 3-4ft (1-1.2m). Plant it in sun or dappled light.

Opposite: *Tulipa* 'Greenland'

Right: The giant rhubarb *Gunnera manicata* grows prolifically in moists soils

Previous page: The tall stems of green calyces are like bells that surround the small white flowers of *Moluccella laevis*.

6 | a rainbow garden

It must be over thirty years ago that I bumped down a rather rutted road beside the Loire in France, a massive château loomed above with a 'garden to visit' sign casually put beside the road. I stopped and entered by a side door and my life changed for ever. I had stumbled on the great potager at Villandry near Tours, a grand early 20th century re-creation of a 16th century French Renaissance *jardin-potager*. Today the garden is reached down a fine road, signposted and with a huge car park, but on that first visit I was there alone. I fell in love with a style of gardening I had never seen before.

A large grid of geometrically shaped beds were immaculately planted with regimented vegetables, outer beds brimming with hot colored flowers and espaliered fruit trees covering trellised fences and arches. The pattern centered on a square pond with cleanly raked gravel between.

This bravura display has its historical roots in the monastic gardens of medieval Europe. During the Dark Ages these gardens kept horticultural traditions alive behind high walls where monks cultivated basic fruits and vegetables and tended herb beds for flavour and medicinal needs. They were gardens shrouded in multi-layered symbolism, the eye of God looked down on beds laid out in grids to the shape of the Cross, the gardens were symbols of paradise, of man's triumph over nature, tiny oases of knowledge in a dark warring world. Physically the gardens were enclosed either by a high woven fence, a hedge or a wall to provide protection and shelter and to allow vines or espaliered fruits to be trained. A well, pond or fountain often marked the center of the garden; water was a symbol of life as well as a convenient place to water the plants from, and for the cook's ready supply of fresh fish.

Below: From his Gothic cage the white peacock surveys espaliered peach trees, cauliflowers, bolting lettuces, white kale and strawberries

Opposite: Profusion in the potager at Kennerton Green

Previous page: Summer bounties in the potager at West Green House

From traditional to modern

Traditional monastic gardens were predominantly laid to vegetables or herbs, with a few flowers permitted as long as they had culinary, medicinal and symbolic as well as decorative uses. The iris, for example, had many virtues: its roots gave perfume and ink, its leaves were used for thatching, and its white beauty symbolized virginity. It joined the rose and lily – the flowers said to be all that was found in Mary's tomb – which became the approved Christian flowers.

The mysticism is wonderful but what first enchanted me was the realization of just how decorative vegetables become when planted in this way, and the possibilities of plant combinations. Making a potager is like making a giant rag quilt with interlocking squares of fruit and flowers, herbs and vegetables. And this pattern can be changed twice a year in hospitable climates.

I have now made four potagers; my first was basically a herb garden at the farm at Burrumbuttock, New South Wales, a walled courtyard that trapped the blistering heat. My next was a major effort on a sub-tropical island north of Sydney, its soil pure sand, the water table only feet below the surface, and worst of all, overhung by huge gum trees that leached any nutrients out of the soil. But it was decorative and productive, its geometric beds overlooked by a hexagonal garden shed, its focal point a dovecote of great charm.

I was in high monastic fervor when the potager at Kennerton Green was laid out. It is quite large 50ft x 50ft (16m x 16m), laid out as a St George's cross intersected by St Andrew's cross, and enclosed by three 6ft (2m) walls espaliered with Red Delicious and Jonathan apples that form lines of brightly colored fruit in autumn. The fourth side is bordered by a long low building with

Gothic design windows behind which strut well loved peacocks. A second lower fence across the path is espaliered with peaches, plums and apricots enclosing the whole garden.

I modelled the Kennerton Green potager entrance on the lychgate of our neighboring church. With subterfuge in mind, late one afternoon the gardeners departed to the church, measuring sticks in hand, to be temporarily interrupted in their work by a vicar intrigued to learn our plans for his lychgate! Its roof is wide enough for shelter with benches to sit on and its ecclesiastical design enhances our theme.

Gates or doorways leading to enclosed gardens are another interesting element in a garden. These could be solid timber doors, plain or carved wooden or metal gateways. The USA is a great source of ideas for decorative vegetable gardens and their traditional style of a simple gate in a white picket fence looks sharp and spruce around a potager. Doors with grilles are very atmospheric, but as long as your entrance can be shut to protect the crops from predators, it can be as dramatic or as simple as the design suggests.

Left: The lychgate at Kennerton Green is a replica of the entrance at St Simon and St Jude's church in neighboring Bowral, New South Wales

Opposite: Artichokes and bean sprouts seen from the Moon Gate at West Green House

Productive parterres

Potager designs can be as simple or as intricate as desired, but a few practical design thoughts help in enabling the garden to run smoothly. Paths can be of any material, gravel, paving stones, compressed earth or sand. In wetter climates old bricks or paving stones are perhaps the best choice. Traditional cobbles are lovely but not easy to push a barrow along and paths must be wide and smooth for ease of maintenance.

If a potager is enclosed within a hedge of cypress, yew or beech, make a path inside the hedge so the roots do not rob the soil of the adjoining bed. Living walls of fruit trees, grape vines or roses are decorative and more practical as they don't rob moisture and nutrients in the same way.

Geometrically shaped beds must be big enough to contain a mixture of a few species of vegetables and flowers, edged in either evergreen perennials or annual plantings. I have had success with annual parsley and marigolds but best of all for me are low 1ft (30cm) high box hedges, or chives. Potagers are basically infilled parterres, so in winter and early spring the design of a box or santolina-edged parterre holds its pleasing pattern until it becomes a riotous joy later on.

Fruit cages designed by Oliver Ford provide the central vertical element in the potager at West Green House, filled with standard bushes of berry fruits with topiaried red, black and white currants and gooseberries underplanted with strawberries

Chives make excellent edging plants, and will always look good if the row is wide enough to be harvested in strips. In a large potager they can be as wide as 20in (50cm), leaving one third of the width always flowering, one third growing and one third just cut. In a smaller situation treat the border as two strips only, trimming the chives less regularly.

Height

I like to have vertical elements in a bed to give height and interest to what are generally quite level plant designs, so any bed should be big enough for a centerpiece, perhaps a wigwam of beans, peas, sweet peas, a standard rose or a 'Ballerina' apple tree whose single straight trunk will be clustered with fruit in season. In France the traditional vertical element is often a model rooster on a stand made from tin or clay, guarding neatly hoed and well tended plots in grids of four or eight beds that supply much of a family's need.

Balls of lavender or rosemary, bay trees topiaried as lollipop shapes, or artichokes in pots can be used to achieve height and style in potager beds. Giant arches loaded with grapes or berry fruit make both practical and stylish high centers for larger beds. Even a clump of sunflowers or corn form excellent center verticals. If the bed is too small, however, it will look contrived, and it is certainly not practical to have oversized elements, for potagers should be practical as well as ornamental.

Bold colors

Color schemes for vegetable garden designs need to be bold and imaginative. Very early in the season at Kennerton Green I plant the central St George's cross with onions interplanted with tulips. One year I included the bold double raspberry and white striped *Tulipa* 'Carnaval de Nice'. Adjoining plots were planted with decorative cabbage, all frilly pink and grey-green, with 'Red Drumhead' winter cabbage behind a confection of purple and blue. Behind these I planted a five colored heirloom silverbeet, also known as rainbow chard, with stems of red, yellow, white, pink and bicolored for a harlequin effect.

As the season progresses tiny faces of heartsease smother my beds, hiding the bare spots left from harvested vegetables. Then the soil is prepared for late summer eggplants, another heirloom mix in whites, lavenders and pinks.

I grew up in a boarding school in Melbourne, Australia where every day from summer to winter we were fed a plate of lettuce with salad vegetables floating on top. So salads have become my least favorite menu choice, with lettuce at the very bottom of the list, but to grow lettuce and all its derivatives is an entirely different matter, for in my eyes nothing looks so beautiful as straight lines of leaves from the palest green to dark bronze-red, veined leaves, ruffled leaves, two toned leaves, long leaves, large flat leaves, miniature leaves, every leaf to make the most satisfying color paths to delight the eye and every other person's palate.

Use all colors and shapes together to form a lettuce carpet. Some 'reds' to try are 'Cerise' with its leaves of bronze-red intricately frilled (known as oak leaf shape) from leaf edge to base. 'Lollo Rosso' is a reliable lettuce that can be planted year round – a green lettuce an extravaganza of frilled bronze red on its lacy edges.

Another year I might plant chard with bright red stems and crinkly leaves the blackest of red to back the red and white tulips. This bolt of color adds an exciting element of surprise. I could choose to coordinate the ruby chard with 'Lollo Rosso' lettuce and perhaps 'Purple Ruffles' basil the reddish-purple fluted leaf variety that is much larger and more arresting than the more unusual sweet basil. The onion 'Brunswick' has the reddest of skins, and the red list continues with the almost regal-purple beetroot, the burgundy Brussels sprouts 'Falstaff', 'Aster Purple' broccoli, radishes, and in warm climates you can grow shiny red capsicums in all shades and shapes of red and cayenne to make a brilliant red vegetable garden. It is a delight to see the dashing colors of onions and beetroot emerge as the vegetables break through the surface of the soil. Add a scattering of black and red poppies and 'Scarlet' sweet peas on poles and by midsummer the vegetable bed becomes true fire.

For the fun of it I once planted at Kennerton Green a bed of the darkest colors interplanted with white, christening the garden 'The Garden of Good and Evil'. The black tulip 'Queen of Night' was interplanted with white leeks and this was backed by a planting of white and purple 'Violet Queen' cauliflowers bordered by my favorite black-red chard. As the tulips faded the black Viola 'Midnight Runner' wove between the leeks and by summer the deep burgundy sweet pea *Lathyrus odoratus* 'Beaujolais' had climbed the central poles beside the hollyhock *Alcea rosea* 'Nigra'. The black French bean 'Sutton's Purple Cream' proved an excellent choice to climb a grid of tripods. The black 'Sweet Chocolate' capsicum and 'Black Russian' tomato, with purple sage and purple basil, became fashion foils in late summer for smart white zinnias. Other fun black vegetables for warm gardens are the slate-purple sweetcorn 'Blue Popping Corn', 'Long Purple' eggplant, a dark glossy purple-black vegetable, and the flat purple podded pea.

Opposite: *Tulipa* 'Carnaval de Nice' gives a
splash of color in the potager alongside young
cauliflowers and kale

Above: Pink and white kale
bordered by chives

Right: The dramatic contrast of
red and green in ruby chard

Giant golden pumpkins, curious gourds and long narrow squash are the knuckle dusters of the late summer vegetable patch, treasures that hide under enormous green leaves, but when grown in raised beds of woven hurdles made from pliant native saplings, these exotic shapes are at eye level, a delight to behold and easy to pick. Raised beds were features of medieval gardens and are both practical and charming additions to traditional potagers. Mine are set out in spring when seedlings of bright golden chard, the pale orange cauliflower 'Marmalade' and seeds of heirloom orange, yellow and white carrots are drilled in lines between the already flamboyant *Tulipa* 'Flaming Parrot', all feathered petals of yellow, orange and red. As summer progresses lines of polished gold and orange capsicums and trained bright yellow 'Golden Sunrise' tomatoes fight a war to try and stay above tendrils of the orangey nasturtium 'Whirlybird' It is the season for giants as runner beans like 'Crusader' with bright red flowers scale up trellises beside 6ft (2m) tall stands of golden yellow sunflowers and ears of yellow corn. The fine filigree heads of *Angelica archangelica* capture the early autumn sun in heads often 12in (30cm) across and tall red fennel becomes a giant skeleton as winter approaches.

Potagers are labor intensive and I tend to fill whole areas with one perennial plant to help save time, especially if all beds are in use. My English potager has enough space to supply a small village with produce, so to make it more manageable and to add decoration I have planted whole areas of one herb placed in a pleasing pattern. Rows of santolina cut into grey balls or maze-type designs

created with two different varieties of lavender have worked well using *Lavandula angustifolia* 'Hidcote' and *L. stoechas* interplanted with rows of box. I have interwoven different sages to make an embroidery of purple, mauves and silver-greys. Carpets of thyme can imaginatively make patterns across unused beds, and mats of strawberries can cover space and smother the weeds. There are many different types of suitable strawberries to use, the tiny alpine strawberries, as well as the white flowered early fruiting 'Emily' and late strawberry 'Sophie' varieties.

One appealing story tells that in medieval times each monk's plot in the potager was identified by a specific type of rose so I like to include roses in a potager design – standards are good for height and climbers for over arches and gateways. Here I tend to favor rather brash colors, the burnt orange of the modern *Rosa* 'Belle Epoque', and the extraordinary striped orange and yellow of the modern *R.* 'Oranges and Lemons' looks dynamic among these autumn-toned vegetables and the strident marigolds – the sunniest flowers for any potager. They sometimes look out of place in the herbaceous border, but can give panache to a seasonal quilt of color in a productive vegetable garden.

Opposite: The flame colored tulips dress the onion patch in early spring

Above right: Late summer flowering sunflowers give a last burst of brightness

Right: Midsummer madness as nasturtium, beetroot, carrots, onions and snapdragons struggle for supremacy

rainbow favorites

Lettuces

The easiest of all vegetables to grow, there are lettuces in shapes and colors to suit most beds in a potager, and varieties that will crop in all but the coldest weather. Mix types for contrast and effect. 'Rouge d'Hiver', is dull bronze with oval leaves, 'Lollo Rosso' and 'Cerise' are frilly reds. 'Great Lakes' is a large hearted pale green butterhead, 'Susan' a stunning bright green, and 'Freckles' is pale green smudged in brown. Try cos lettuces such as large leaved mid-green 'Lobjoit' or tiny 'Little Gem' for their vertical light green leaves. Cut-and-come-again varieties include the bright light green 'Lollo Biondi'. For red-brown hues, try 'Bronze Arrowhead' with its arrow-shaped leaves. 'Deer's Tongue' has slim elegant pale green leaves with rounded ends.

Cauliflowers

You need no longer be satisfied with white curds surrounded by ruffles of blue-green leaves. Now you can grow 'Esmereldo' with its bright green curds, deep purple 'Violet Queen' or even pale orange-leaved 'Marmalade' with tiny contasting white heads.

Chard

Chard comes in a range of the most amazing colors. Rainbow chard is pure fiesta adding fun, light and drama to any vegetable garden and it is very hardy and will thrive in drier conditions. Planted in spring it will crop all summer and even if it does tend to bolt I leave it in just to enjoy its fiery color. Stems of bright orange, lemon and gold look magical planted near lines of marigolds,

trailing nasturtiums or at the feet of flame colored dahlias and as a foreground for the round-faced sunflowers. Stems of pink, white-lemon and 'blue' produce a partytime look, and all taste good.

Beans

I like beans that look like candy canes, especially, 'Barlotta Lingua di Fuoco' with bright red splashes on a light green bean. 'Cosse Violette' is a deep purple, and 'Corono d'Oro' is pale gold and string-less, making beans a colorful vegetable to grow.

Globe artichoke

If you have a reasonable amount of space the majesty of the long silver-grey leaves makes globe artichokes among the most elegant and structural addition to a vegetable garden. Flower heads add a further bonus as giant lavender thistle heads reach for the sky but once this display is over in summer cut back immediately then by autumn the silver-grey leaves are as beautiful as ever. Artichokes like rich soil and long drinks of water which is to be expected as in three months the plant grows from a seed to a plant over 5ft (1.5m) tall.

Sage

The hairy oval grey-green leaves of sage are invaluable in any garden, and a welcome addition to any winter border. In the potager try weaving together a selection of varieties of fragrant culinary sage *Salvia officinalis*. *S.o.* 'Purpurascens', the purple sage is lovely when combined with the golden leaved *S.o.* 'Icterina' and *S.o.* 'Tricolor' with its variegated leaves in white, green and pink.

Sage bushes tend to become spidery so prune hard after flowering, but they are hardy survivors in poor soils.

Sweet peas

Climbing up wigwams or against walls and fences, spilling over embankments, sweet peas are associated with cottage and kitchen gardens, stiff-stemmed flowers of enticing perfume. Available in white, cream, all shades of pinks, reds, lavender and purple and nearly black they are a joy to pick in early summer and last a week or so indoors. Sow old-fashioned varieties such as the purple-blue 'Matucana' or pink and white 'Painted Lady' for maximum scent. Sweet peas are easy to grow but need sunshine and watering when young. They will not grow in very hot climates. Sow into fertile well-drained soil or compost in containers, and don't go overboard with too much tender care or you'll end up with excessive leaf growth and few flowers.

Kale

From late winter to early summer the frilly leaves of the ornamental cabbage in shades of pink, mauve and white or variations of each are pure decoration in the garden or vegetable garden. Beautifully structural shapes, I use them extensively in the early spring potager. Plant out in late autumn in warmer climates, late summer for cool areas, but it is not a plant for the tropics. To keep them in the garden as long as possible cut the flowers as soon as they appear and keep cabbage moths at bay.

Opposite: Nasturtiums climb alongside the red flowered runner beans to create a tangle of rainbow colors

Above: *Coreopsis* are pure summer sunshine flowering until the autumn. I like them especially at the feet of sunflowers

Opposite: *Echeveria,* its pearly grey sheen a subtle source of light, is pure stylised beauty as a mass of it overflows in urns

Previous page: The old stable walk at West Green House was once shadowy unforgiving surfaces of old cobbles and bricks. Today pots of spring and summer flowers, climbing hydrangeas and roses capture every ray of light to create a soft and colourful walkway

I have been fortunate in gardening in several completely different environments where the local colors have impressed upon me the need to work with the demands of a landscape.

One of the most imaginative gardens I've ever seen was a Provençal hillside garden. This was a living sculpture in shades of grey-green filled with hundreds of native Mediterranean plants, the color so soft above the white soil and rocks of Provence. These were subtle forms in a bright white light, compact plants curved against the hillside, moulded into shape by the strong winds of the Mistral. This was a garden perfectly in tune with its environment.

Mediterranean plants are now the vogue for excellent reasons: they are drought-resistant, mostly non-invasive and many are the herbs we treasure for flavor and fragrance. But before transferring the same ideas of color and planting schemes to a different situation one has to ask whether the dull grey of Mediterranean native plants would look so pleasing under skies that are for months just shades of grey, where the soil is of a stronger color, or in urban landscapes? Before selecting any plants one has to consider the color of a new environment.

Look at the local landscape to find inspirational ideas for beautiful tones in the garden. In Provence the late Madame de Vesin took as her starting point the color and form of the surrounding vegetation. Around her were soft greens and greys picked out by the whiteish stones of the rocky hills. So, by designing her memorable garden in various shades of blue, olive and white, she cleverly reflected the colors of her environment.

Tumbling from grey urns in sun drenched European courtyards like smooth shining petals carved from blue-grey stone, the perfect rosettes of pearl grey echeveria species are polished grey foliage plants that look romantic when grouped together and spilling over a sculptural shape. Being light reflective plants they add color and light contrast in dry areas of somber filtered shade. Echeveria are sun loving plants that tolerate shade, yet they are also perennial succulent and evergreen subshrubs that are easy to grow in temperate to subtropical climates as long as they have good drainage. The white sheen on the grey-green leaves seems to look contented in many environments and their appearance brings to mind groups of open roses, frozen as ancient fossils in time.

Working with local color

Nearly thirty years ago I went to live in sheep country in southern New South Wales. There the elements controlled the farmers' livelihoods. Temperatures seesawed from 90 degrees plus day after hot summer's day to bitterly cold winters. Rain, or the lack of it, was the main topic of conversation in the church yard on Sunday; grave heads noted who had received the most and commiserated with those the clouds had passed over. The soil contained red pigment, which provided a harsh canvas of bold color quite unrelated to the soft background colors of a garden in the cooler areas of the northern hemisphere, for the red earth captured and retained the hot sun, causing pastel shades to fade, and the colors of rich pinks to drain away. Only in pools of purple shade could they look really fresh .

A local building material was a red clay that contained blue, an unforgiving color that was nonetheless practical in withstanding the staining dust and mud. Old homesteads were often surrounded by orchards of apricots, quinces, peaches, cherries and almonds and groves of citrus trees. They were strands of polished green forming deep-shaded restful circles of dusky blue and mauve that were cool oases lit by shiny fruit of orange, yellow and lime, refreshing light and colors redolent of a climate of extremes.

Bright clear colors look designed for the reddish earth, and my first country garden was an early lesson in finding plants and colors to suit the demands of the land. Roses loved it, laid out on the red soil across a gravel ridge exposed to the winds, a sieve for water to drain through. The catalogues in those days featured mainly hybrid tea roses, heritage roses remained in old gardens loved by those that knew them but unavailable to the average gardener. The English roses were still to come. So to create my colors I turned to *Rosa* 'Sutter's Gold', a deep gold, *R.* 'Grandpa Dixon', a good yellow, cream and pink *R.* 'Peace' and the floribunda *R.* 'Apricot Nectar', sprays of soft apricot-yellow. The neon orange *R.* 'Super Star' shone as a youthful enthusiasm. I might choose none of these colors now, but in their setting they seemed entirely right.

'. . . in my memory
the sun is
always shining
there,
the bright light
dancing off water
and leaves,
a chip of
sapphire in an
azure sea.'

Daisy-style flowers grew simply by placing a cutting in the ground with a minimum of water. *Euryops pectinatus* grew into 4ft (1.2m) grey-green bushes with ferny leaves covered with golden-yellow daisies. Yellow centered white marguerites *Argyranthemum frutescens* and *Anthemis tinctoria*, the ox-eye chamomile, grew in soft mounds. *Fraxinus excelsior*, the golden ash tree, and the claret ash *Fraxinus angustifolia*, were tolerant of the dry climate and looked exciting beside beds of purple, lavender and yellow. The native mint bush *Prostanthera ovalifolia* was temperamental but covered with delightful small purple flowers, and it joined varieties of grey leaved cistus with mostly white flowers; *Lavandula dentata* and the lilac pin cushion *Scabiosa caucasica* intermingled with purple and white mealy sage *Salvia farinacea*, the toughest of plants. The twin mopsheads of white and blue South African agapanthus were the mainstay of midsummer, and brilliant birds gorged on the red, orange and yellow berries of the autumn *Crataegus*. My garden was an assembly of colors of the Mediterranean, but it was far from a Mediterranean garden.

In the dry wheat belt the Australian gums cast a shade of deep purple and blue reflected from color deep in their grey leaves. In spring this shade is lit by the golden light of the flowers of the *Acacia baileyana*, the native Cootamundra wattle, one of the most vivid varieties. In our garden we grew *Acacia baileyana* 'Purpurea', its lacy silver-grey foliage tipped in purple providing a garden color code for a spectacular border of plants, echoing the color of our surrounding vegetation.

Shades of blue-purple with clear yellow and gold are strong and vibrant in any light. Among the most successful planting schemes are the dark silvery-blue sea holly *Eryngium bourgatii* 'Oxford Blue' reaching above groups of *Helichrysum italicum* clipped loosely to form silver-grey balls with tufted flowers of yellow in summer. Or try *Achillea* 'Taygetea', its flat saucers of tiny yellow flowers on stiff stems above a blue-green ferny foliage. Another crescendo suggested by bush color could comprise mounds of *Nepeta* 'Six Hills Giant', a lavender-blue flowered perennial with lax grey leaves, with *Aster* x *frikarti* 'Mönch', a vibrant lavender Easter daisy.

Our surroundings can dictate the colors we should use around us. I once had a house on Dangar Island, a speck in the estuary of the Hawkesbury River, an hour north of Sydney. It was a tiny community where the hour of the day was judged by the putt-putt sound of the ferry echoing from the river, and the mournful call of the native mopoke brought shivers to the soul. The island is engulfed in a blue landscape, tented by blue-grey eucalyptus, surrounded by sea and sky of the clearest blue. It was there that I first grew a blue and white garden. From the verandah overlooking the water there was nothing to see but stark blue and white flowers and wistful fronds of subtropical green plants; these were the colors of the surrounding landscape. The seashore was blue and it was this blue light I aspired to reflect in my plantings.

Banks of the pale blue *Plumbago auriculata* that flowers all summer scrambled down the embankment to the beach. The hardy blue agapanthus was tucked into the meanest spots, and large bushes of *Ceanothus* 'Blue Pacific' rivalled the sea in an intensity of blue. White spider lilies grew under tree ferns, palms and rioting white and purple bougainvillea, and drifts of fragrant star jasmine. The 'floor' was a mass of the Hawkesbury River daisy (sometimes called the Swan River Daisy), *Brachyscombe multifida*, large cream gazanias and the bright blue daisy *Felicia* beside long green frangipani leaves and banks of darkly polished *Gardenia augusta*. It was the most rampant garden I've ever planted, a blue jungle creeping ever closer. The pruning knife lay beside my pillow. It was an uncomplicated happy garden, a garden for a summer's place in the summer of my life.

Eventually I sold that garden, when I fell under the spell of West Green House, and in my memory the sun is always shining there, the bright light dancing off water and leaves, a chip of sapphire in an azure sea.

Few of us can play with an entire landscape, but it is easy to light shady spots with shiny evergreens, especially those with white flowers. A dark corner in a small garden can be brought to life with a generous evergreen such as Fatsia – its sharply cut shiny leaves attracting attention into a mysterious shady area. Or plant soft white and cream flowers alongside the palest blues · to bring added light to a small North European garden.

Opposite left: I cannot grow a garden without South African agapanthus in a dry Australian summer. The strappy leaves are polished green and the erect flowers in blue or white are the epitome of freshness on hot days

Opposite right: The tiny blue daisy-shaped *Felicia* will create summer blue carpets in cool Mediterranean climate gardens

Above: It seems that no respectable rose garden is complete without *Nepata*, but I prefer it amongst plants of yellow and acid lime

Using the colors of walls and buildings

I sometimes wonder how relevant gardens will become as more people live in urban communities, city centers where the environment is the color of steel, glass, concrete and granite, the materials used to clad the buildings of the 21st century. Grey-stained contours control the movement of wind, light and shade, creating microclimates where any plant or garden must match the environment they provide, bare dark pockets of shade or sun traps of unrelenting heat. As new tall buildings arise to cope with growing urban population, changing the environment, creating new wind tunnels and areas of dense shade, town gardens are often forced to abandon traditional lawns and borders, to try new designs and styles.

Urban landscape architects contrive a myriad of stylish ideas to bring color and pleasing life into these hard-edged landscapes, great sheets of water to capture sky, sculptured landforms to reintroduce grass, color in man-made materials. Many are emerging that are simply paved areas interspersed with hard-edged pools, plants just narrow green boundaries. But many plants also suit urban drama, offering living shafts of light in dark corners, bold splashes of color against the greys, soft shapes against the angles. Living walls, for example, offer welcome light and life, stylish urban boundaries include walls pleached with *Magnolia grandiflora* or espaliers of shiny leaved camellias or evergreens used as hedges, cut to the required heights.

Small urban gardens offer their own possibilities for playing with light, for example in a garden surrounded by buildings or high walls the light will be directed and trapped into quite specific areas. Try using dramatic containers as spotlights to capture and reflect this light, planting them with a striking centerpiece such as a yucca with softer shapes and colors of annual plants of your choice tumbling over the edges. Wherever they are placed the eye will be directed that way, so place containers at different heights to highlight different spots. And use obelisks, pyramids or sculptures to draw attention to different areas, and if your walls are too dark to grow climbers of your choice successfully decorate them with eyecatching lightcolored or metallic objects. Curiously, the most striking colors for garden structures in a dark garden are often dark shades such as sage green or even black.

An attractive permanent planting for long lasting color in a container could consist of the spiky blue grass *Elymus magellanicus*, and the bright yellow woolly leaves of *Stachys byzantina* 'Primrose Heron' with *Sedum spathulifolium* 'Cape Blanco', rosettes of grey-blue with sulphur yellow flowers for summer to autumn light.

The stable walk at West Green was long and drab and used to be quite spooky, a narrow walkway overshadowed by tall buildings of mossed red bricks, and a pathway cobbled in stones of a dark hardness. It needed informal tall and broad pots planted with soft tumbling plants to add color, light and lightness, so to achieve this I placed three pots each a quarter full with soil, one on top of another. The basepot 27in (65cm) diameter x 22in (50cm) high, the middle pot 18in (45cm) diameter x 16in (40cm) high, and the top pot 14in (35cm) diameter x 12in (30cm) tall. Each summer in soft apricot to complement the bricks, trails of *Verbena*

'Peaches and Cream', spreading *Viola* 'Antique', *Nicotiana* 'Salmon Pink' and bushes of the bluest lavender I can find, join the powder blue *Lobelia erinus* 'Cambridge Blue', *Nepeta nederifolia variegata* and white marguerites to form a 4ft (20cm) fall of gentle profusion in white, apricot and blues.

Color for me is as important on the small canvas

Below: The man, his spade and his duck beside the tall obelisk have symbolically turned their back on this world. A monument to a head gardener at West Green House is a focal point of light color amongst the green

Opposite: Against the oldest walls the pale cream, yellow and pink spidery flowers of *Lonicera* x *americana* complement the color of the aged bricks

of a wall as in an entire landscape. When I arrived at West Green House only four climbing roses remained on the house, one was the buff-yellow Noisette rose *Rosa* 'Gloire de Dijon', with three plants of a rich mid-pink blossom, apparently bred by David Austin and known as the 'West Green Rose'. This was a beautiful rose, but against the warm orangey-red brick it was a violent statement, while the old *R*. 'Gloire de Dijon' buff touched by gold and pink softly melded into the ambience of the house.

All the roses close to the house are now different vintages of champagne: *Rosa* 'Alchymist' is a golden-yellow climber, *R*. 'Céline Forestier' is the lightest primrose on light green leaves, a Noisette rose *R*. 'Gardenia' is a Wichuriana rambler and *R*. 'Mme Jules Gravereaux' a buff-yellow climbing tea rose. Single cream and white roses with pronounced stamens, such as *R*. 'Sir Cedric Morris', a rampant mass of tiny flowers on soft grey foliage, and *R*. 'Cooperi Burmese' (*R. laevigata*) are large dramatic cream-white flowers, again with long stamens, that will climb and cover a whole wall. All are enhanced by the glow from these old walls but the rose that gives me most joy is *R*. 'Madeline Selzer', a rambler, her perfect off-white flowers touched with lemon on pale green pleated foliage, a perfect foil for the microcolor climate she now inhabits.

Grey walls can provide neutral backgrounds for experimentation with any color. The quintessential old world image is an explosion of every shade of pink, a melody of crimson to pastel in roses, clematis and honeysuckle cascading down walls of grey. It is the imagery of the striped pink petals of *Clematis* 'Nelly Moser' intertwining through a rambling *Rosa* 'Madame de Sancy de Parabère', a blending of pinks with a smidgeon of lavender. Or it conjures up a picture of the Wichuriana rambler *R*. 'Evangeline', its clusters of delicate posies of small single white flowers, blushing pink rapturously entwined in a vigorous *Clematis montana* var. *Rubens*. This clematis will bound away from constraining supports to conquer telephone poles and wires, throughout the warmer spectrum of cool temperate areas.

On a shady wall, an alternative to roses and clematis is the strong self-suckering climber *Hydrangea petiolaris*, its flowers forming a mass of frothy lace in spring, with broad green leaves making a soft green wall carpet until autumn. In a very dark spot try one of the many ivies splashed with cream or yellow, but remember that a little ivy goes an awfully long way, and this rampant plant is generally best as a backdrop to bring some light to a very dismal corner. It is easy to tire of the bold shades of variegated ivies if they are not used subtly.

Opposite: Roses of parchment, cream and warm sunset are lit by bricks of ochre and red. Here, *Rosa* 'Glorie de Dijon' scrambles up the walls of West Green House

Above: *Clematis* 'Nellie Moser' looks beautiful intertwined with mauve-flushed roses

Below: The rich pink West Green rose – a vigorous climber looks best against walls of white or grey, or trained to be seen against the sky

Shade houses

In the new world grey walls tend to be weathered paling fences, or occasional concrete brick walls, but in old settlers' gardens there are still bush houses (shade houses) made of hundreds of grey weathered slats, the smartest ornamented with intricate fretwork. Here the harsh light is filtered through on to treasured collections of plants.

To step inside the half light of tropical shade, pushing aside cobwebs and vines into the decaying gloom of a Victorian bush house, passing tiny pools of water creating sticky humidity, brushing back palm fronds covering modest statues, is to gain a century old lesson in the beauty of filtered light a total contrast to the strongest light outside. If you gaze at an old photo of a low built verandered house, built on a ridge surrounded by sand dunes in the deserts of the far west of New South Wales, you see how the bush house alongside allows filtered shade to protect treasured plants from scorching heat and inland frosts, allowing a green plant to survive in a totally different light and climate zone to its natural habitat. Colonial bush houses contained the desired plants of the period, collections of palms, ferns, orchids and fuchsias scarcely different from those found in English conservatories of the same period. My grandmother's bush house in the desert landscape was completely crammed with ferns. On her death they came overland to us, huge baskets of maidenhair fern, *Adiantum,* plus three or four other species, always to be kept away from frost and daylight in filtered light with moist feet.

Few people are lucky enough to have shade houses these days, but a shaded conservatory or similar will do just as well. Trailing 'tassel fern' *Lygodium* forms an attractive double-fringed lace curtain hanging down from baskets. They need good drainage, as does the 'Hen and chickens' fern *Asplenium bulbiferum*, another reliable fern for indoor shade houses. Place bird's-nest ferns *Asplenium australasicum* and *A. nidus* above eye level in a decorative pedestal urn where the large light bright shiny sword leaves will look strong and architectural among the lace of other ferns and the height will hide their messy centers.

Many vines in warmer climates are so rampant that they make nonsense out of arches and decorative supports, and create shade houses all by themselves, fashioning perfect walls and ceilings out of the most basic supports to create several story structures to show off their brilliant flowers. The heavily scented *Jasminum polyanthum* with its shell pink star flowers above pointed buds of crimson-red that can encase a small building, is gentrified when intertwined with the leather leaves of the *Hoya carnosa*, a plant often treated in cooler climates as especially tender but I've found can be quite aggressive once it becomes established. The flowers look like wax posies frozen in time under old glass domes that emerge from five sided wax packet shaped buds, the color of ladies' corsetry. Spiders love this plant and if in a prominent

Cool green fronds of *Adiantum* lend soft texture and light to the darkest and hardest sufaces

Previous page: A small grove of acers, Japanese maples, are sheltered from strong sunlight at Kennerton Green to turn all the colors of autumn

'. . .a century old lesson in the beauty of filtered light. . .'

position I tend to want to clear its leaves of their dust covered webs, so these climbers are best smothered in a tangle of other vines. This leads me to a story I must tell. When I arrived at West Green House, a 1720s orangery was glassless but still provided shelter for a number of camellias to survive, though they were obviously not as highly regarded as two pots deeply shrouded in frost proof cloth. I asked what they were, and whether I might look. No, I was told by the then gardener, they were special plants and would perish in England's midwinter cold. I prevailed and was eventually allowed a peep, whereupon I collapsed with laughter. For only 24 hours before in Australia I had paid a workman yet again to try and remove a row of stubborn oleanders that refused to die, while in England they were the treasure of the shade house!

Shade cover

By midsummer lawns in hot dry climates do not survive under a canopy of deep green shade so I have turned there to a hard landscape pattern, a grid of sandstone paths to correspond to the size of the shade cover. The squares within the grid are filled with shade-tolerant ground cover plants such as the bronze-leaved blue-flowered *Ajuga reptans* 'Jungle Beauty' and the old-fashioned sweet violet. Although these are often associated with the image of mossy banks, they are really quite adaptable and need water only on the hottest days. *Ophiopogon planiscapus* 'Nigrescens', a slow-growing grass of black-bronze looks sharp in squares juxtaposed next to its green brother *Ophiogogon japonicus*. These plants contrast in shape and texture too, the grasses both rather narrow and fine, the other plants with a more rounded leaf shape.

Rather than struggling to maintain a herbaceous bed in a shady spot, discover instead the advantages that more architectural ideas can provide, flat geometric shapes filled with different ground cover shade plants or simply with hard landscaping materials can look particularly effective – interesting in a country garden and dramatic in a townscape. A good solution for contemporary urban gardens is to make a grid of square beds that are just blocks of evergreen hedges or single plantings. I suggest blocks of the small leaved evergreen laurel *Prunus lusitanica* which are excellent in hard area. 'Lace cap' hydrangea *Hydrangea macrophylla* and *Azalea indica* 'Alba Magna' are both reliable hardy plants for dappled shade.

Colored light

Pagodas, trellised walks, trellis across terraces or pergolas, all create pools of colored light in a garden. Look up into a trellised ceiling of falling racemes of laburnum or wisteria and it is looking into colored light. I grow the softest pink *Wisteria floribunda* 'Kuchi-beni' , with its long waterfalls of flowers 4-18in (10-45cm) long that pale to white in stronger sun, or try *Wisteria floribunda* 'Honbeni' , the better known deeper pink wisteria that's sometimes called 'Rosea' with its rosy glow. The plant is not as floriferous or reliable as 'Kuchibeni' but provides showers of pink sun in early spring light.

Aged figs trained and pruned to cover trellis cast pools of deep green shade, as do the wide leaves of grape vines in Mediterranean climates and the pruned plane trees that verandah French terraces. The Australian backyard passionfruit vine is deep shiny green with dull purple fruit, when tied high to simple wires it also provides dense cool green light in summer. A summer's day viewed from beneath an awning of green makes a bright day even more sparkling, and the last warm days of summer are unforgettable when sitting under the fiery leaves of an autumn-coloring vine such as *Vitis davidii*, creating a painted room of memorable reds and golds.

When planning a garden, if you have the space for trees don't forget the vibrant autumn colors of those such as the pistachio *Pistacia chinensis*, an autumn flame in cooler climates with leaves all crimson, orange or scarlet. A grove of acers light a row of dark crypresses like fire at Kennerton Green and the sugar maple *Acer saccharinum* is unsur-passed for color in cooler districts. In my Australian garden *Nyssa sylvatica*, a tall pointed tree, turns the kitchen orange as the sun pours straight through it on autumn afternoons, and a waterside group at West Green House casts red light on the new lake. Although slow growing trees, nyssas are a must have if you have the temperate climate and space to grow them. Try and choose beautiful deciduous trees that do not stress and drop sad early browned leaves as summer refuses to end – *Liquidamber styraciflua* do well in many climates their leaves turning all shades from the deepest plum to red, gold and yellow, holding onto the tree while others are totally bare. Ash trees can also be relied on to perform: *Fraxinus excelsior*, the golden ash and *F. angustifolia* 'Raywood', the claret ash, individually create pools of deep gold and ruby red light.

Right: A young *Wisteria sinensis* drapes over the forecourt arcade at West Green House

Opposite: In spring simple terracotta pots hold winter violas and early flowering tulips. Small pots of green box also soften the hard surfaces

Contrasting light

In classical gardens light has often been brought to long tunnels or walls of green by objects, pale statues, urns , obelisks, columns, sculpture and ornamental fountains. The light captured in white stone is a dramatic foil for dark foliage, a shaft of light like a diamond encrusted pearl shining out from a little black dress. One special summer at West Green I filled the large urns placed in the all green theater with a growing flower arrangement. Height came from the tall leaves of the cream and green striped leaves of *Phormium* 'Cream Delight' and transplanted pots of spiky leaved yucca, all the mature plants capped like the Matterhorn's peak with bells of white. Drooping plants of white marguerites and trailing geranium spilled over the sides, the bowl was then crammed with the Asiatic lily *Lilium* 'Apollo', grey helichrysum and fuschias completed the confection that bloomed to be a romantic centerpiece of soft white light against deep green yew hedges.

Urns in entry courts, courtyards and front gardens are often the focus of attention by night and day. Flowers of dark blues and purples 'die' under artificial light but light blue backed by clear yellow, lime or pale green looks light and inviting under hot sun, shade or lanterns. A large urn planted in simple clear yellow such as the fringed 'Maja' tulip or the tall 'West Point' lily-type tulip with masses of blue forget-me-nots, would be clear light in a still grey garden of early spring.

Each winter I place plants of box or holly clipped into interesting shapes in urns by the front door. These stylish vessels replace highlights of seasonal color with an elegant form of shiny green. These shapes cast dramatic effect when backlit by the house lights that are nearly always on in the darker time of the year.

8 | sparkling light

On my first trip to Italy I drove from Rome through frantic traffic one hot July day to arrive at yet another car park where the dusty gravel exploded in powder puffs when I stepped on it. A garden path began immediately to descend into an underworld of green gloom where giant terraces were carved from a hillside completely encased in eiderdowns of moss. Laser shafts of sunlight pierced the green canopy above lines of playing fountains, capturing every droplet of water like thousands of glittering sequins, lighting the terraced gardens with pinpoints of tiny lights in a dark green night. The renowned gardens of the Villa d'Este gave me an unforgettable lesson in the power of water to light a garden.

When you have the chance, sit beside a clear meandering stream and see how the water dazzles in direct sunlight, but glitters in broken light. Or look at a deep still pond where water lilies decorate the surface; it will appear calm, but the serenity is broken by the life around the lilies. Their shiny leaves act as light reflectors, and the minute insects hovering and dipping around them flick the surface water to create pinpoints of broken light.

Lighting with water

Many gardens must conform to a rectangular sized general block of land. My beach cottage garden on Dangar Island was this shape. The island is a beautiful place, still well covered by stands of tall eucalyptus trees and lying in the mouth of a wide river whose high banks are virgin bush. I wanted to capture its spirit in the back garden which was heavily shaded by mature gum trees and the lavender-blue *Jacaranda mimosifolia*. I needed to capture light on water to compete in some way with the brilliance of the sea beyond the front door. So a lazy S-shaped stream was made to meander through the garden, the water emptying into a lotus pond by the back door. The water was reticulated by a simple pump but as the stream passed over the uneven bush rocks it captured the sun's rays escaping from overhead foliage – firstly from the gums and jacaranda trees, then through citrus and then a streamside planting of spectacular Japanese iris, tall papyrus grass and a collection of spreading dwarf maples, mostly *Acer palmatum* and *A. palmatum* var. *dissectum* varieties. The water created a ribbon of silver life, at least as beguiling as the drama of the open sea beyond.

All types of iris look designed for planting near water. Above the water on dry paths or embankments the bearded iris *Iris germanica* is completely at home. The most accommodating of plants, they thrive with a few handfuls of slow release fertilizer and lime but need the sharp cold of winter for good flowers. Daylilies are even more considerate, happy from the tropics to cool climates with midsummer flowers in a continuous succession after only general garden care. Lousiana iris are true glamour for warmer climates, they are happiest in water but bloom in marginal plantings. If you can possibly grow them, do! Japanese iris seem designed for man made reticulated streams that are turned on to flow in spring and summer as this iris likes dry winter feet. In midsummer tall graceful leaves back huge blooms some as big as 12in (30cm).

'... the tulips nodding above a dancing light, the sparkling light reflected from the uneven water surface of the rock lined rill.'

Left: **The tall spikes of iris are not only wondrous flowers but their silky texture captures and reflects the sunlight**

Above right: **The peony-style *Tulipa* 'Angélique' shimmers in the light from the tiny stream of broken water**

Previous page: **Water catches the eye and leads it to the old stone steps and through the gates into the walled garden**

Lifting shade with water

A subtle yet eye-catching stretch of water now lights what was originally a very predictable long bed of spring bulbs at Kennerton Green. This corner of the garden was a random collection of the usual bulbs and blossoms of spring, built up over the years and pushed out into the garden as time and money allowed. As the trees grew their canopy thickened overhead and the bulbs began to give more leaf than flower, so that the spring sunlight becoming completely captured in the huge mass of blossom. So it was time for a facelift, the garden beneath needed captured light, it required back lighting to help the bulbs to compete on equal terms with the theater above.

The entire length of the bulb-bed was lifted and a rill 275ft (85m) long now splashes over uneven bush rocks into four ponds, reflecting and playing with the light. The bulbs rather than the rill were to be the feature, the purpose of the rill was to provide a mysterious sparkle, its source to be discovered only if visitors cared to look carefully. At the height of spring it is completely hidden by flowers – the tulips nodding above a dancing light, the sparkling light reflected from the uneven water surface of the rock-lined rill.

By midsummer the bulbs are cleared away and it becomes the time of the hostas clustered close to the rill – an eclectic collection, a sampler of all shades of green from pale green and yellow to leaves rimmed with gold and white, an admirable sight until we are outmanoeuvred in our eternal battle against the snails. The rill then changes from a lighting extra to the leading lady in this part of the garden, its ribbon of light a glittering show which emphasizes the shapes and sizes of the hosta leaves, distracting from the leaves of the heat-stressed trees above.

A rill is an easy way to add sparkle to a garden of virtually any size. All that is needed is a small pond with a return tank for a reservoir, a trench lined with a black polythene membrane then covered by rocks or pebbles, a pump and a supply of water – this could be the garden hose. Before switching the pump on each spring make sure your pond and water tank are filled, then top up from time to time as the water slowly evaporates.

Hostas are five star plants forming rounded clumps of beautifully shaped and colored leaves happy in the darkest moist corners, in filtered light, but they scorch in full sun in all but the coolest climates. *Hosta sieboldiana* has huge pleated leaves of blue making clumps often 5ft (1.5m) across. *Hosta crispula*'s oval leaves are edged in white and look particularly good as underplanting for green and white tulips in early spring, creating a river of white light under the shade of trees. *Hosta fortunei* 'Aureomarginata' has yellow-green splashed around large deep green leaves, golden highlights to echo the color of any golden shade tree above. *Hosta* 'Gold Standard' has heart-shaped gold leaves just tipped in dark green, the best gold highlight plant of all!

Adding drama with water

Once the brambles were cleared in my English garden, I was able to walk for the first time through the beautiful 19th century Moongate, to glimpse on a rise above a large grey wall in classical style. On its crumbling façade some words of the 18th century poet Alexander Pope were carved: 'A little learning is a dangerous thing. Drink deep or taste not the Pierian spring'. From beneath these words water had once flowed from a devil's mouth into an urn that overflowed to a basin. Further away a waterless rill stopped in a pile of grey stones that had been placed to look as though they fell like water into two parallel ponds. The concept was all wonderfully allegorical but visually it was grey and disjointed.

Today it is a true water garden to complement the imposing Nymphaeum folly, with water descending down steps cut into the natural slope, catching the light and diffusing it. It is a garden of green, white and silver – a glittering display of light and water enclosed in an allée of yew trees cut at stepped heights. The water trickles from the mask to the urn, the basin and the tank, appears in the rill, then glides down wide shallow steps as a large sheet of moving mirror capturing the cool northern light, reinforcing the classical serenity of the grand design. The water reappears as smooth as glass in the ponds, then

Opposite: The new narrow rills of water bring moving light to the old steps at West Green House

Right: A fine ribbon of water pushes through old box and is an arrow light pointer in the newly planted Nymphaeum garden

cascades down beside the old uneven steps as a light filled stream inviting exploration of this sparkling garden.

Levels in even the smallest garden or courtyard create interest, a sense of space and an element of style. A change of levels means that steps can be placed in a focal point, and that their center can be channelled out to make a small water feature which trickles down the middle. Try planting a small sharply clipped hedge against the risers of the steps; a hedge with 'blue' tones such as rosemary *Rosmarinus officinalis* will tolerate a dry position, and so too will box, *Buxus sempervirens*, or severely clipped *Lonicera nitida* for little hedges of small green leaves. The water in the tiny channel will create flickers of light depending on the lining. Marble can provide a smooth creamy-white light while pebbles give a darker broken light catching any light and diverting the eye to the garden.

Water features enthusiastically installed in gardens so often become horrible mosquito ridden bog patches when forgotten or overgrown with rampant aquatic plants, but a water feature that is a fountain will still look beautiful even if unused and abandoned. A small bronze fountain was placed in the center of Kennerton Green's vegetable garden, of a small putti surrounded by shells, a frog and a tortoise. Water drips from these features into a pond below now blanketed in miniature bright pink water lilies, but for most of the day the putti is colonized by the fantail pigeons who have realized this is the nearest supply of fresh water to their cote. Totally unplanned, the snow white birds perched in the fountain above the pink water lilies has become one of the most enchanting spots in the garden. We made the rim of the pond a ledge wide enough to sit on to recover after hoeing a row of vegetables, and it is a favorite spot to watch water droplets catch a ray of light that breaks up into millions of sparkles as they fall into the water lilies below.

Still water and mirrored light

Light in all its forms can be captured in any still pond. In secret or enclosed parts of a garden a pool can become a charming mirror as long as the light can reach it. At Kennerton Green a long flat pond in the rose garden captures the color of the sky from above the tall hedges and reflects the pale colors of the standard roses which run alongside. The water provides glorious reflections when the flowers bloom, but maintains style and interest in all seasons.

Modern urban gardens often include water to draw down the light. However the often angular pools are usually left unplanted, relying on the water to be the feature, although in very shaded areas water catches the most light if planted with light-reflecting waterlilies *Nymphaea* and water iris or with stylish lotus *Nelumbo* in warm climates. Shade ponds can look murky and easily become wells for wind swept debris, stagnant and unattractive if left without reticulation or plants to oxygenate the water.

Troughs

In the Bay Tree garden at Kennerton the geometric planting of dull leaved trees is now being lit by a long trough of reticulated water falling over copper cut at different lengths to capture not only facets of light but to make musical sounds. Many Australian gardens have smart pools and fountains made from water troughs placed against walls with all types of beautiful objects used to feed water to them. Easily constructed from bricks to the size required, the sides and ledge of the trough can be surfaced with Haddonstone blocks, sandstone, marble, granite or rendered cement, often to match materials used in house construction, the liners of metal inserts of the same size. Carved dolphins, lions and urns or decorative taps may be used to feed water into this increasingly favored garden accessory. Often these troughs are features of courtyards where the sound and the light playing on the moving water creates the impression of coolness and life in areas that sometimes become hot dry suntraps.

Left: Light is captured and shines from rills, steps and ponds in a newly created space

Right: Droplets metamorphose into pure light bringing even the dullest surfaces to life

Opposite: A perfect example of still water that has become a mirrored surface reflecting all the surrounding light

'. . . a fleeting
morning
of white glitter,
a perfect reason
to set out
another
parterre next
spring.'

Winter sparkle – water frozen as ice or
snow creates garden embroideries in
winter, pictures of white ice etched over
dark green as the outlines of a parterre or
clipped santolina become tablecloths of
white lace. The light of these delicate
traceries after a hard frost must be one
of the most exquisite sights a gardener
can plan for, a fleeting morning of white
glitter, a perfect reason to set out another
parterre next spring.

Reflecting light in glass and glazes

Brilliant glass mosaics and glazed ceramic tiles can capture prisms of colored light into an arched covered walkway where light is dim and plants cannot grow. Or use mirrors for trompe l'oeil effects in a small garden to give the impression of light and distance. In my Australian garden I have introduced cheerful light into an awkward space by inserting into two niches hand painted folk tiles whose brilliant color tells the story of St Francis and the birds. A more formal approach to attracting light appears high in the walls of West Green House where 300 years ago General Hawley had the busts of Roman emperors placed, lifting the eye to their round niches of white giving light to a plain wall and fantasy to a small house.

In enclosed courtyards a mirror placed on a wall can capture and reflect light into bleak corners. A necessarily short path can appear to lead into infinity by taking it to a wall mirror. Or follow the advice of garden designer Rosemary Alexander and create a successful illusion by placing a gate in front of a wall mirror, a beautiful gesture to attract us to continue walking into this space of light.

In town gardens problematical neighboring walls can be turned to advantage as perfect backgrounds for all types of wall plaques. Museum shops stock excellent classical copies or do as I did, collect folk tiles whilst on holiday to make an attractive story in brightly glazed tiles, especially those with crazed finishes that break up and reflect light. I still have a shoe box of folk tiles hoarded away to insert into a path one day. The

loud sharp colors of ethnic wares are an excellent foil in a pathway of plainstone, cement, brick or terracotta. Dropped in randomly or in sequence they bring bright light, color and conversation to very pedestrian constructions.

I must admit that in church my eyes tend to roam to the sorrowful inscriptions on the walls. Those on the brightly polished shiny brass surfaces immediately draw the eye, the bright metal attracting the eye, making the black lettering stand out. So in a garden a shiny object will capture every ray of sun, attracting us like moths

to a light. I've only used two shiny objects, a sun dial and sphere at Kennerton Green now darkening with age, and now not so brilliant, but bright enough to break up light adding captured sun to a still garden. A metal plaque with lines of treasured poetry placed on walls or in paths again captures stray beams of light. I like the idea of finding a verse when weeding a garden, it gives a pause for reflection, the light in the metal subtly illuminating the surrounding scene.

American friends had told me about the Seattle artist Dale Chihaly's glass sculptures for

gardens. Last summer his exhibition of pure vermillion glass poles was placed into the main borders of Government House, Sydney. Like tall slim poles from which Venetian gondolas moor, they were for me fantastically exciting garden objects, pure cylinders of vermillion internal light. This large assembly of poles was definitely for a major area but a small group in a contemporary garden would be magic giving perpetual colored light against a deep green sculptural garden or providing glowing slashes of red light in the grey light of winter.

Ground light

The choice of paving in a garden can drastically effect the light and the mood. Pristine white gravel chips, for example, can bring lightness and light to heavy corners when spread along a shaded path, but sometimes this effective way to reflect light can be overwhelming. I arrived for the first time at the cottage at Kennerton Green, in February – our hottest month, and remember very clearly coming to the kitchen at midday to wash the lunch dishes. The kitchen overlooked a pristine white gravel car park that was a blindingly brilliant square, giving off an incredible glare. In the bright sunlight a calming solution was needed to create an oasis of restfulness and serenity in an area of jangling brilliance. I solved the glare by planting a small parterre to offset the light, a simple clean design of dark greens to absorb the brilliance. It showed me that dazzling effects must be controlled like a few sequins or jewels in a greater story.

Different materials react very differently to light, soft grey or sandstone paving slabs are subtle in cool northern light, allowing plants spilling over onto the surfaces to proclaim their own glory, or creating a low level light contrast when adjacent beds or pots are planted with silver or grey foliage plants. Cobbles or patterned bricks allow light to dance on their different surfaces, gravels should tone with the color of adjacent buildings or other structures, bouncing light off each other. Intricate patterns and mosaics in ceramics and stones can provide interesting light effects in a small area; evergreens look very stylish against white gravel or marble chips.

> . . . a shiny object will capture every ray of sun, attracting us like moths to a light.'

Opposite: The marble white image of a Roman emperor lights a bare wall lifting the eye to its niche

Left: Old garden implements sprayed white are a bright statement on the old mottled pink walls in the orangery

There are a myriad of garden ideas and styles to select from. Clever books and international travel expose us to a fruit salad of stylistic impressions and plants, so it is often frightfully confusing to know what exactly is a dream garden. As we pass through life the dreams change, the ideal of a long garden with sandpits and swings becomes swimming pools and decks for smart parties. Dreams of grand gardens of classical serenity give way to quiet courtyards in sunny climates as the needs of our age change. So everyone will have different dreams. For many work will necessitate years in apartments in foreign cities, a wind swept balcony or a patch of unloved grass in a forgotten yard, the closest suggestion of green.

Some day a garden will come along, but wherever it is sit and comtemplate the sky, the countryside, the everyday culture and they will supply the clues for a beautiful garden full of light and color.

Previous page: *Allium bulgaricum* – tall stems of greenish-white bell-shaped flowers broadly striped with red brown